The Ontological Argument of
Charles Hartshorne

American Academy of Religion
Dissertation Series

edited by
Mark C. Taylor

Number 20

The Ontological Argument of Charles Hartshorne
by
George L. Goodwin

George L. Goodwin

The Ontological Argument of Charles Hartshorne

Scholars Press

Distributed by
Scholars Press
PO Box 5207
Missoula, Montana 59806

The Ontological Argument of Charles Hartshorne

George L. Goodwin
The College of Saint Catherine

Library of Congress Cataloging in Publication Data

Goodwin, George L
    The ontological argument of Charles Hartshorne.

    (Dissertation series - American Academy of
Religion ; no. 20 ISSN 0145-272X)
    Originally presented as the author's thesis,
Chicago, 1976.
    Bibliography: p.
    1. God—Proof, Ontological—History of doctrines.
2. Hartshorne, Charles, 1897-   I. Title.
II. Series: American Academy of Religion.
Dissertation series - American Academy of Religion ;
no. 20.
BT102.H363G66 1978   231   78-2821
ISBN 0-89130-228-X pbk.

Printed in the United States of America

1 2 3 4 5

Edwards Brothers, Inc.
Ann Arbor, MI 48104

FOR SCHUBERT M. OGDEN

TABLE OF CONTENTS

Page

TABLE OF ABBREVIATIONS   ix

FOREWORD BY CHARLES HARTSHORNE   xi

INTRODUCTION   xix

CHAPTER I: A STATEMENT OF THE THESIS   1

   1. Hartshorne's Ontological Argument   1
   2. Logical Considerations   2
   3. Philosophical Considerations   8
   4. A Statement of the Thesis   10

CHAPTER II: THE METAPHYSICS OF TEMPORAL POSSIBILITY . .   13

   1. Hartshorne's Understanding of Metaphysics . . .   13
   2. Two Central Metaphysical Doctrines   21
   3. Logical Features of Hartshorne's Metaphysics . .   31
   4. Hartshorne's Theory of Temporal Possibility . .   34

CHAPTER III: POSSIBILITY AND DIVINITY   51

   1. Classical and Neoclassical Understandings
      of Divinity   52
   2. A Formal Ambiguity in the Notion of Perfection .   57
   3. Perfection Requires Potentiality: the
      Metaphysical Arguments   60
   4. The Existence-Actuality Distinction   64
   5. Conclusions   73

CHAPTER IV: POSSIBILITY AND MODALITY   77

   1. Necessary Existential Statements   78
   2. The Connection Between *De Dicto* and *De Re* . . .   79
   3. The Intelligibility of *De Re* Modality   83
      3.1 Quine's Argument   84
      3.2 The Smullyan Reply   89
      3.3 Modality *De Re* and Hartshorne's Argument .   94
      3.4 Kripke Semantics   97
      3.5 From Semantics to Metaphysics   101
   4. Summary   114

CHAPTER V: A SUMMARY OF THE ARGUMENT   119

BIBLIOGRAPHY   129

TABLE OF ABBREVIATIONS

The following abbreviations for Hartshorne's works are used in the text:

MVG   *Man's Vision of God and the Logic of Theism.*
Chicago: Willett, Clark & Co., 1941. Reprinted by
Archon Books, 1964.

RSP   *Reality as Social Process: Studies in Metaphysics
and Religion.* Glencoe, IL: Free Press, 1953. Reprinted by Hafner Publishing Co., 1971.

PSG   *Philosophers Speak of God* (with William L. Reese).
Chicago: University of Chicago, 1953.

LP   *The Logic of Perfection and Other Essays in Neoclassical Metaphysics.* LaSalle, IL: Open Court,
1962.

AD   *Anselm's Discovery: A Re-examination of the Ontological Argument for the Existence of God.* LaSalle,
IL: Open Court, 1965.

NT   *A Natural Theology for Our Time.* LaSalle, IL: Open
Court, 1967.

CS   *Creative Synthesis and Philosophic Method.* LaSalle,
IL: Open Court, 1970.

WP   *Whitehead's Philosophy.* Lincoln: University of
Nebraska, 1972.

FOREWORD

I congratulate Dr. Goodwin on the lucidity and fidelity of his exposition of my form of ontological argument. Not only has he understood me well, but he has (in Chapter IV) strengthened my position by dealing with some relevant controversies in recent formal logic that I have not touched upon.

If I were asked, "Why do you believe in God?," I would not reply, "Because of the ontological argument." Rather, I would say that it is because of a group of arguments that mutually support one another so that their combined strength is not, as Kant would have it, like that of a chain which is as weak as its weakest link, but like that of a cable whose strength sums the strengths of its several fibers. (I have developed this theme in the chapter on "Six Theistic Proofs" in my *Creative Synthesis and Philosophic Method* [LaSalle, IL: Open Court, 1970], pp. 275-97. This essay first appeared in *The Monist* 54 [April 1970], 159-80.) None of these interrelated arguments were properly stated until recently, and one reason for this was the failure to understand the argument of Anselm; for it is this argument that gives us the clue to the logic of any possible theistic argument. As has always been realized, Anselm's argument is non-empirical, but what it shows, if anything, is that any possible theistic argument must be equally non-empirical, and so must any anti-theistic argument. The distinctiveness of the ontological argument is not that it is conceptual or modal rather than observational, but that it assumes as consistently meaningful the idea of deity, whereas other arguments assume other ideas and seek to show that the idea of God as necessarily existent is implied by these other ideas, which, it is argued, are strictly indispensable and applicable not only to the actual world order but to any conceivable one, any coherently thinkable reality.

I wish here to summarize once more the gist of the ontological argument as I view it. We have known since Leibniz that the necessary is what is common to a set of possibilities (for which, as Goodwin shows in Chapter IV, "possible worlds" is a somewhat misleading label). To be necessary is to be implied by the actualization of no matter which of the set of possibilities in question. If the set is all possibilities whatever, all that is genuinely conceivable, then the common aspects are unconditionally necessary. Only unconditional necessity is relevant to Anselm's argument. Hence the a priori status of the argument.

It follows from the foregoing that, to know what necessity is, we must know what possibility is. If, as I hold, logical possibility implies something about reality as such, then so does logical necessity, in spite of what Hick and some others have claimed.

What is logically possible? If we reply, "Whatever can consistently be thought," "can" repeats the modal problem. What indeed can be thought? A thought is always about something other than just itself. The idea of God is not the idea of the idea of God. Consistent thinking is not simply about itself as consistent thinking. Whether or not "man-headed horse" is a consistent idea, its elements, "man", "horse", "head", are intended as references to kinds of products that nature or "the creative advance" have produced or are capable of producing. Clear away all reference to the temporal process and its actual or conceivable products, and you may suppose that you are still thinking coherently; but I see no reason to accept such a claim. (I am not forgetting pure mathematics.) Language is never merely about itself and thought never thinks just itself.

Why is it supposed that logical possibility tells nothing as to real possibility? The answer is not far to seek. In any given here-now, creativity is narrowly conditioned by what has been happening, including those regularities or laws of nature that have characterized the happenings and are presumably still in force. In asking about the logically possible we abstract from the here-now and the obtaining laws and ask what the creativity can consistently be thought of as producing, not here-now but somewhere and somewhen, and according to conceivable laws, or absence of law if that is conceivable. Or we ask, "What is the creativity itself?" (But then we are asking, "What is necessary?") The limitations upon creativity as

xii

operating here-now are thus set aside. What limitations are
left?

The answer depends upon how the regularities or laws referred to are conceived. If the laws are given the classical
form of Laplace or Kant, then everything in conflict with these
laws is still excluded no matter how far back in time we locate
our "initial conditions." Moreover, in the here-now nothing is
really possible except what actually happens. This is the
strictly deterministic view of causality, the theory that becoming is creative only from the standpoint of our ignorance of
causes since, in truth, the definiteness of nature now was
fully implied by past happenings and their laws. If, however,
we think of laws as Boutroux, Peirce, many other philosophers,
and more and more scientists, have conceived them, then there
are really open possibilities each moment for the next moment,
since laws are irreducibly statistical or approximate. Becoming, on that view, is indeed creative, productive of new
definiteness, not implied by what went before. In this way we
come closer to making logical and real possibility coincident.
Many things made impossible by what persons or other active
singulars have done *were* possible before these actions. The
farther back in time our reference goes, the larger the segment
of logical possibility that will have been really possible for
the future.

There will still be a lack of coincidence between the two
kinds of possibility, unless we take one more step. The laws
of nature, however statistical or approximate, still exclude
thinkable kinds of occurrences from happening. The final step
needed to complete the unification of real and logical possibility is to regard natural laws so far as genuinely contingent
or with thinkable alternatives, as themselves products of the
creative advance, in other words, emergent aspects of reality.
And why not? What could possibly tell us that regularities
obtaining now in nature obtained in all past time and will obtain in all future time? It is hard enough to justify extrapolation from a finite stretch of observed happening to an in-
definitely longer period (as Whitehead puts it, for the dura-
tion of our cosmic epoch), without vainly trying to extrapolate

to infinity. By giving up the futile effort to derive eternal truths from temporal and contingent regularities, we make it possible to regard all contingency as referent to the freedom of creativity to produce, at some unspecified past or future time, whatever is genuinely possible. Not that whatever is thinkable will sometime occur, but that there must have been a time when it was not excluded as a possibility for the future of the creative advance. And so various thinkable laws, other than those now obtaining, must once have been, or may now be, open options for the future (options for God if not for the creatures).

To summarize the foregoing: all thought is about something, never about sheer nothing; the indispensable minimum of what thought is about is creative becoming as always transcending complete causal determinacy with respect to the next moment and transcending even partial determinacy taking the whole past and future into account. On this view contingency comes into the world piecemeal rather than in one wholesale dose, one throw of the dice or divine fiat back of the beginning or in eternity. Accordingly, logical possibility, or what makes sense, is co-extensive with ontological possibility, or that whose production is compatible with the nature of creativity as indispensable referent of all meaning--or, if the assertion is unconditionally necessary, that which is required by that nature.

The reader may have guessed how these reflections are relevant to the ontological argument. God is not in most theologies thought of as a mere possible or actual product of creative becoming; rather he is thought of as indispensable aspect or form of the creativity, other than which, and its manifestations, there is nothing for thought to think, whether as actual or as possible.

A number of philosophers now agree with me that the ontological argument can be given a valid form provided one grants that it is genuinely conceivable, logically possible, that God exists. Suppose this assumption is false, as Carneades long ago and Carnap and others more recently have held it to be. Then the argument does not prove the truth of theism; but it still proves something, namely: neither theism nor atheism can

be contingently true. And this is one of the most important
results ever achieved in the philosophy of religion.

Consider the following quite simple reasoning:
p* for: deity (defined, say, as unsurpassability by another
conceivable being) exists

    (1) Logically possible p*

    (2) (Logically possible p*) implies (logically necessary p*)

    (3) Logically necessary p*

    (4) Therefore p*

    (2) is Anselm's Principle, as I call it.

Only logical modalities are used in deducing the conclusion, which follows from (1) and (2) by modus ponens and the
axiom, necessary p implies p.

The proper modal system (Lewis's S4 or S5?) may be a problem. Also the necessity in question cannot be the narrowly
technical one of "analytic" as defined, say, by R. M. Martin,
since more than logical constants are used in explicating p*.
However, what are used are ideas as little empirical as logical
constants. Also the necessity does fit the broader meaning of
analytic as defined by Hick, that truth follows from the meanings of the terms. It must of course justify the step from (3)
to (4). I believe that all this is consistent with the
allegedly paradoxical axiom of strict implication that a necessary proposition is implied by any and every proposition.

If we deny the conclusion, then by modus tollens we deduce
the contradictory of (1), implying the logical impossibility of
the divine existence.

Ontological considerations enter into the reasoning only
informally, as giving grounds for the premises (1) and (2).
But since this is outside the formal deduction, it cannot re-
lease opponents of the argument, or of theism, from the obli-
gation to reject at least one of the premises.

Hick and many others reject (2) but accept (1). Carnap
and others reject (1), implying that (2), (3) and (4) are ill-
formed, without clear and consistent meaning. I see a case for
this view. What I do not see is a case for accepting (1) but
rejecting (2), thereby affirming the conceivability of the
divine existence and also that of the divine nonexistence.

What is the reference of the latter? It cannot be to the actual history of the world process, for this implies an idolatrous view that God's existence depends upon what creativity produces, rather than being inherent in the creativity itself. It cannot be the incoherence of the idea of deity, for (1) has been accepted. If the idea of possibly nonexistent deity is about nothing, then it has the same content as the idea of nothing, and is not about deity. Is it perhaps about the idea of deity as uninstantiated? But an idea capable of being instantiated and also of being uninstantiated cannot in itself constitute the truth of either alternative. Only a necessary or impossible idea can, just in itself, constitute the truth or falsity of its instantiatedness. So I find nothing that empiricists could be thinking of when they speak of the conceivable nonexistence of deity, taken as also capable of existing. Anselm was right, if God is conceivable, his (or her--language embodies male chauvinism) nonexistence is not conceivable. John Hick's remark that Anselm did not write about logical necessity is trivial. Anselm did ask, "What is (coherently) conceivable?" and this is what matters.

Since, as I have just argued, the only rational way to reject Anselm's argument is to deny the conceivability of God's existence, then either theism is logically necessary or it is absurd or incoherent. It follows that observation of contingent facts is irrelevant to a decision to believe or not to believe. To be sure, necessary truths are implied by any and every contingent fact, but only because of what such facts have in common with any conceivable ones. Hence the famous problem of evil, which argues from the evils in the actual world to the falsity of theism, should be equally cogent were the world as different as you please from what it actually is. And if the heavens declare the glory of God, then so does the career of Hitler. It is an old idea that the believer who cannot see the presence of God in every situation does not see it properly in any situation. Thus observation of historical or contingent facts can never tell us whether or not belief in God is justified. Only reflection upon those ideas which express what all possible observations have in common can do this.

There remains one advantage on the side of the believer. If he understands his belief, he knows that if any conceivable phenomenon could manifest the divine creativity then every actual phenomenon does so. He also knows, on the same assumption of conceivability, that the contingent facts of which he is aware form content of the divine awareness and thereby qualify the divine reality on its contingent side. He knows that our world, with its joys and sorrows, is also God's world. But what can contingent facts tell the unbeliever who understands the issue? He should see that they tell him nothing at all about God, including whether or not God exists. An unbeliever's entire wisdom on the question must come from semantic-ontological understanding of metaphysical first principles. If nontheists do not wish to struggle with metaphysical problems, they had better put the entire matter to one side, as indeed many do. Nor have I any unkind word for this procedure.

It is worth noting that if the ontological proof implies the invalidity of the atheistic argument from the facts of evil, that invalidity can be shown in quite another way. For the argument assumes as deducible from the idea of God a pseudo-idea of omnipotence that analysis shows to be a confusion, a linguistic blunder. This is the notion of one creative power or decision maker with a complete monopoly on decision-making, if deciding means, as I take it to do, selecting among really open possibilities. People say that they "make decisions"; yet God, according to the conventional idea of omnipotence, really makes everything, including all decisions. We merely reiterate his decisions for us, and he can see to it that this is the case. I regard this way of doing theology, copied by atheists for their own purposes, as logically invalid. Decision-making logically could not be monopolized. No decision, taken in its full concreteness, could be made by two agents, even if one of them is God. And if only God makes decisions, then what is the word decision doing in our language? If you ask, "Why did God make it possible for unfortunate decisions to occur?" the answer is, "Because to this possibility there is no alternative." A God making all decisions would have no creatures and nothing significant to decide.

So here too the Anselmian proof helps us to take the right view. If theism is an error, the mistake is in a broad sense logical, and the same holds of atheism.

No logical schema of inference can compel us to believe or disbelieve. But it might help us to set aside mere confusions and pseudoconceptions that have long complicated an issue that is difficult enough without them.

There are other ways than those specified of arguing informally for Anselm's Principle. Dr. Goodwin has competently discussed some of them. Anselm (with a precedent in Aristotle) began a search, only now coming to fruition, for those features that distinguish concepts capable of contingent instantiation from those not thus capable. Examples of the latter are *round-square* and *being something*, the one necessarily without and the other necessarily with instantiation. The theistic issue, as Anselm partly realized he had discovered, is this: does "being divine" belong, in its modal status, with round-square or with being something?

For the rest I commend to the reader Dr. Goodwin's careful and well-written study.

Charles Hartshorne

INTRODUCTION

Is there a single issue that lies at the center of Charles Hartshorne's ontological argument for the existence of God, and, if so, what is it? Hartshorne himself has provided valuable clues for an answer. For example, in *Man's Vision of God* (1941) he wrote that his ontological proof "*deduces* this exceptional status [God's necessary existence] from a generally applicable theory of possibility together with the definition of God. Nothing else is required" (301). In response to a review of that book, he tightened the connection between the theory of possibility and the conception of God, arguing that "the idea of perfection, when coherently defined, *requires* that there be potentiality as well as actuality" (Charles Hartshorne, "The Formal Validity and Real Significance of the Ontological Argument," *The Philosophical Review* 53/3 [May 1944], 227; italics added). In *Anselm's Discovery* (1965) Hartshorne confirmed his earlier judgment, arguing that "possibility itself must be expressive of the divine" (148) and that the divine existence "constitutes possibility as such" (296).

This study is concerned with the systematic exposition and critical evaluation of these clues. The central thesis is twofold: (a) that Hartshorne's argument revolves around two foci, a theory of divinity and a theory of modality, and (b) that the interpretive key to both theories is Hartshorne's metaphysics of temporal possibility. Part (a) reflects two intuitive concerns which almost everyone struggling with the argument has raised: Is not God the great mystery who lies beyond the limits of rational considerations and metaphysical formulae, so that our knowledge of him is chiefly negative? And, even if we could devise a positive conception of God that did not intrude on his mystery, is it not both folly and arrogance to assume that we can argue from our logical conception of such a being to his ontological reality? Part (b) of the thesis addresses these questions by arguing that Hartshorne's metaphysics of temporal possibility not only provides the principles for a reinterpretation of the traditional idea of God which is coherent and meaningful and yet preserves the mystery of the Godhead, but also provides the principles to support the contention that all consistent, coherent and meaningful thought must be about reality.

The study has five chapters: (1) a statement of the thesis, (2) an exposition of Hartshorne's theory of temporal possibility, (3) the employment of that theory in Hartshorne's reconception of the idea of God, (4) the theory of possibility as the key to Hartshorne's theory of modality, and (5) a summary of the argument. The "theory of modality" in Chapter IV will involve us in the contemporary discussion of the *de re-de dicto* issue; specifically, the intelligibility of *de re* modality and its connection to *de dicto* modality.

The study, then, is intended to make both an interpretive and a constructive contribution to Hartshorne scholarship: interpretive, in that it draws attention to a unifying theme (the theory of possibility) in Hartshorne's work on the ontological argument; constructive, in that it employs Hartshornean principles to provide a metaphysical underpinning for *de re* modality. This latter contribution is in accord with Hartshorne's prediction that "the future of the ontological problem lies largely in rather technical developments in formal logic (including modal logic or, perhaps I should say, metalogic)" (AD, xiii).

CHAPTER I

A STATEMENT OF THE THESIS

The purpose of this chapter is to introduce the central thesis of the study: that Hartshorne's ontological argument depends upon a theory of divinity and a theory of modality, and that these in turn depend upon a metaphysics of temporal possibility. Subsequent chapters will explicate that metaphysics and show precisely how it is the interpretive key both to Hartshorne's conception of God and to his theory of modal correspondence.

The outline of the chapter is simple: after (1) an introduction of Hartshorne's argument, I will isolate the assumptions in order to concentrate (2) on the logical structure of the proof and (3) on the philosophical issues involved. I will conclude by (4) stating the thesis in relation to this analysis.

1. Hartshorne's Ontological Argument

We may begin by examining the formalized version of Hartshorne's proof which he presented in *The Logic of Perfection*:[1]

'q'	for	'(∃x)Px' there is a perfect being, or perfection exists
'N'	for	'it is necessary (logically true) that'
'∿'	for	'it is not true that'
'v'	for	'or'
'p → q'	for	'p strictly implies q' or 'N∿(p & ∿q)'

1.	q → Nq	"Anselm's Principle": perfection could not exist contingently (hence the assertion that it exists could not be contingently but only necessarily true[2])
2.	Nq v ∿Nq	Excluded Middle
3.	∿Nq → N∿Nq	Form of Becker's Postulate: modal status is always necessary
4.	Nq v N∿Nq	Inference from (2,3)
5.	N∿Nq → N∿q	Inference from (1): the necessary falsity of the consequent implies that of the antecedent (Modal form of modus tollens)

6.	Nq v N∿q	Inference from (4,5)
7.	∿N∿q	Intuitive postulate (or conclusion from other theistic arguments): perfection is not impossible
8.	Nq	Inference from (6,7)
9.	Nq → q	Modal axiom
10.	q	Inference from (8,9)

As with all proofs in philosophy, two questions are relevant in regard to this argument: is the reasoning logically valid?, are the premises true? The answer to the first question is affirmative, since the proof follows standard rules of logical theory. I am unaware of any comments to the contrary in all the literature reviewing the argument.

Given a formally valid proof, rejection of the conclusion must entail rejection of one or more of the premises. "Thus," as Hartshorne writes, "a proof establishes a price for rejecting its conclusion, and in this way clarifies the meaning of the latter" (CS, 276). Our attention may, therefore, be profitably and correctly directed to the second of our questions: are the premises true?

Hartshorne identifies the assumptions in his argument (LP, 51) as: (1) the first premise, q → Nq, which he calls "Anselm's Principle": the statement "a perfect being exists" is, if true, necessarily true; (2) the third premise, which is a form of the strong reduction principle of modal logic: modal propositional status is always necessary; and (3) the seventh premise, ∿N∿q, which asserts that the existence of a perfect being is possible. Strictly speaking, we may also add to the list of assumptions the modal axioms operative in the argument, steps 5 and 9. Rejection of the conclusion, therefore, will entail rejection of one or more of these five assumptions. I turn now to an investigation of each.

2. Logical Considerations

2.1 *The Modal Assumptions*

Under this heading I include the third, fifth and ninth steps of Hartshorne's argument. Two of these assumptions we may regard as self-evident. Step five is the modal form of

modus tollens: if one proposition strictly implies another, if
the second is necessarily false, then so is the first. Step
nine is the consequence *a necesse ad esse*: if a proposition is
necessarily true, then it is true. These axioms seem obvious
enough.

The third step, which is a form of Becker's Rule or the
strong reduction principle, distinguishes Lewis' S.5 system
from more moderate or weaker systems of modal logic. I offer
these two observations concerning the strong reduction principle: In the first place, Becker's Rule does seem intuitively
plausible. The Rule says that propositional modal status is
always necessary, so that, for example, $\Box p \rightarrow \Box\Box p$, $\Diamond p \rightarrow \Box\Diamond p$,
$\sim\Diamond p \rightarrow \Box\sim\Diamond p$, and so forth. Since every proposition is either
necessarily true[3] (true in all possible worlds), or necessarily
false (false in all possible worlds), or neither necessarily
true nor necessarily false (true in some possible worlds, false
in others), it seems obvious that for any arbitrarily selected
proposition, the modality it does have it must have, and the
modalities it does not have it could not have. What would it
mean to call a proposition necessary if it could be contingent,
or to call a proposition contingent if it could be necessary or
impossible? If, for example, p is contingently true in this
world, this is because it is false in some other possible
world, say W_1. How then could it be necessarily true in any
possible world; for if it were necessary in some possible
world, say W_2, its necessity would by definition mean its truth
in every possible world. Therefore both $\sim p$ and p would obtain
in W_1--but this is contradictory. In short, it is necessary
that p is contingent in every possible world. Similar arguments
in reference to the other two modalities lead to the same conclusion: propositional modal status is necessary.

In the second place, we can present Hartshorne's argument
without employing the strong reduction principle. Anselm's
Principle (which we will examine below) says that *if* God exists,
he exists necessarily, so that the statement that he exists is
necessarily true. Hartshorne has symbolized this as: $q \rightarrow \Box q$.
However, Anselm's Principle can be equivalently formulated as:
the existence of God is either necessary or impossible, so that

the statement that God exists is either necessarily true or
necessarily false. Or, in symbols, $\Box q \vee \Box \sim q$. Using this formulation, then, we may construct the argument thus:

1. $\Box q \vee \Box \sim q$ Anselm's Principle
2. $\sim \Box \sim q$ assumption
3. $\Box q$ inference from 1,2
4. $\Box q \rightarrow q$ modal axiom
5. q inference from 3,4

In an excellent analysis of Hartshorne's argument, R. L.
Purtill has employed the three modal axioms in Hartshorne's
proof to derive a theorem which underscores the proof's central
logical thesis. Purtill demonstrates that from the following
three principles of modal logic:

1. $\Box q \rightarrow q$ (Hartshorne's ninth premise)
2. $(q \rightarrow r) \rightarrow (\Box \sim r \rightarrow \Box \sim q)$ (modal modus tollens, Harts-
                        horne's fifth premise)
3. $\Diamond q \rightarrow \Box \Diamond q$ (a form of the strong reduction
                        principle employed in Harts-
                        horne's third premise)

we can derive the theorem, $(q \rightarrow \Box q) \supset (\Diamond q \rightarrow q)$, which is to be read:
If a statement is such that if it is true at all then it is
necessarily true, then if that statement is possibly true then
it is true.[4]

This theorem formalizes succinctly the interior logic of
Hartshorne's ontological argument. That proof turns logically
upon the unique relation between the actuality and the possibility of God. Once it is realized that necessary existence is
analytic of the very idea of God (Anselm's Discovery), then it
follows that any possibility of the divine existence necessitates actual divine existence. Aristotle expressed this insight when he wrote that "with eternal things to be possible
and to be are the same" (*Physics*, III, 4.203[b], 30). More recently, J. N. Findlay has put the point this way: "The possibility of a necessary existent is no ordinary possibility, precisely because it is not a possibility if it is not also more
than one, i.e., an actual fact."[5] Or, in Hartshorne's words,
"If he is not less than a possibility, he can only be more,
that is, an existent" (MVG, 314). *If it is the case that if*

*God exists, he necessarily exists, then any possibility of the
divine existence necessitates actual divine existence*: this is
the logic of the ontological argument.

To this principle, Hartshorne adds two assumptions:
(1) q → □q, if God exists, he exists only necessarily, and (2)
∿□∿q (= def ◇q), it is possible that God exists.

2.2 *Assumption:* q → □q

Hartshorne names this assumption "Anselm's Principle" or
"Anselm's Discovery" in honor of *Proslogium* III, where Anselm
argues that "it is possible to conceive of a being which cannot
be conceived not to exist; and this is greater than one which
can be conceived not to exist."[6] Or, more briefly, necessary
existence is superior to contingent existence. The presupposition behind this principle, that *modality* of existence is a
predicate, is, Hartshorne contends, logically independent of
and philosophically superior to the suspect principle of *Proslogium* II, that real existence is greater than mental existence,
and to its underlying presupposition that existence is a predicate (which Kant so effectively challenged).[7]

Anselm's discovery may be formulated in various ways: *if*
God exists at all, he exists only necessarily; God could not
exist contingently, so that his existence is either necessary
or impossible; God can be conceived only as existing necessarily. All the formulations make the same point: that *necessary
existence is analytic of the idea of God.*

Suppose that we deny q → □q. That is, we deny that if the
statement, "a perfect being exists," is true, then it is necessarily true. This amounts to asserting, by the definition of
strict implication, the denial of ∿◇(q·∿□q), that is,
∿∿◇(q·∿□q), or ◇(q·∿□q). Substituting (∃x)Px for q, we have
◇((∃x)Px·∿□(∃x)Px), or the equivalent statement,
◇((∃x)Px·◇∿(∃x)Px). This amounts to saying that it is possible
that a statement affirming the existence of a perfect being is
true, and yet it might be false.

Hartshorne contends, however, that the proof is not open
to precisely this objection. "Perfect being" has been defined
so as to include the notion of necessary existence, and in this

way we rule out contingency of existence or non-existence. The only viable options are necessary existence or impossible existence.

It may seem that we are justifying such a central assumption in Hartshorne's argument too easily by *fiat*. But consider: in the first place there is nothing *prima facie* absurd or inconsistent about defining God or "perfect being" so as to include necessary existence, and in fact there are cogent theological and philosophical reasons for supposing that the divine existence could not be merely contingent. What would it mean, for example, to say that, although God now exists, there was a time when he did not exist, or there will be a time when he does not exist? This would be theological nonsense, for one of the chief characteristics distinguishing God from creatures is that God does not pass into or out of existence like contingent beings.[8] His existence is strictly necessary.[9]

"If God exists, he necessarily exists" is a logical truth as well. Alvin Plantinga, for example, argues that "it is plausible to suppose that the maximal degree of greatness entails *maximal greatness in every world*. A being, then, has the maximal degree of *greatness* in a given world W only if it has *maximal excellence in every possible world*."[10] But maximal excellence in every possible world entails existence in every possible world, and this is just the definition of necessary existence. So we are on solid ground when we insist that *if* God exists at all, he necessarily exists.

In the second place, not only is Anselm's Principle faithful both to the Judaeo-Christian theological and to the philosophical uses of "God," that principle carries the additional advantage of focusing attention where it ought to be focused in the ontological proof, namely, on the assumption that the existence of God is possible. The question is not whether we can deny that *if* God exists, he necessarily exists (for we rule out that denial by definition), but whether we can legitimately assume that the idea of a perfect being makes sense, that is, whether the existence of God is even possible. "The only place to halt the argument, to insert an if, is where the logical positivists halt it, prior to the assumption of a meaningful concept. Once that is granted, possibilities, alternatives, drop out, since perfection has at most but one intelligible status, existence."[11]

2.3 *Assumption:* $\sim\Box\sim q$

How we conceive and interpret the idea of a perfect being makes all the difference in the outcome of the ontological proof. If we can coherently conceive the notion, then we have just the possibility which necessitates the divine existence; and if we cannot coherently conceive the idea, then it is possible--and, by the ontological proof, necessary--that God does not exist. The argument can cut either way, for or against theism.

The assumption that the existence of God is possible is, Hartshorne holds, the central axiom in the argument and the one most difficult to justify. He contends, in fact, that the Anselmian, and indeed the entire classical metaphysical understanding of perfect being as *actus purus* is incoherent, and so turns the ontological argument into a cogent proof of the necessary *non*-existence of God. (J. N. Findlay has used the argument in exactly this way.[12]) A great deal of Hartshorne's writings, therefore, is devoted to giving the notion of "perfect being" an intelligible and coherent "neoclassical" reinterpretation. Chapter III of this study will be devoted wholly to presenting and defending that reinterpretation; consequently, I will not pursue justification of this assumption further at this point. Simple identification of the assumption will suffice for the present.

2.4 *The Purtill Version of the Proof*

I have been isolating and identifying the assumptions operative in Hartshorne's proof: the modal axioms, from which Purtill derives the theorem, $(q\to\Box q) \supset (\Diamond q\to q)$; Anselm's Principle, $q \to\Box q$; and the assumed conceivability of deity, $\sim\Box\sim q$. We may thus follow Purtill in presenting a shorter and simplified version of Hartshorne's proof:[13]

'q'	for	'(∃x)Px,' there is a perfect being, or perfection exists
'□'	for	'it is necessary that' or '∿◇∿'
'◇'	for	'it is possible that' or '∿□∿'
'p⊃q'	for	'p materially implies q' or '∿(p & ∿q)'
'p→q'	for	'p strictly implies q' or '□∿(p & ∿q)'

1. (q→□q) ⊃ (◇q→q)   theorem
2. q →□q   assumption (Anselm's Principle)
3. ◇q → q   1, 2, M.P.
4. ◇q   assumption (perfection is conceivable, i.e., logically possible)
5. q   3, 4, M.P.

The advantage of this version of the proof is that it reduces deductive transitions among the steps to a minimum, and so sets the assumptions in bold relief. Any questions about the conclusion will have to be directed either to the first, the second, or the fourth step. And, as I have pointed out, since the first step derives logically from axioms in modal propositional calculus, and since the second step simply reports accurately on correct theological and philosophical uses of "God," questions as to the truth of the premises ought to be addressed chiefly to the fourth step, the assumption that the existence of God is possible.

3. Philosophical Considerations

When we inquire as to the truth of the assumption that the existence of God is possible, we quickly involve ourselves in two large philosophical issues: (1) the possibility and types of concepts of God and (2) the relation of thought to reality.

The logical mainspring of the argument, to state it once again, is that in one unique case, possibility necessitates actuality, because *mere* possibility of existence cannot apply to a being whose existence is, by definition, either absolutely necessary or utterly impossible. Obviously, then, the argument must justify the assumption that the definition of a necessarily-existing being makes sense, that is, that the concept of God is a coherent and meaningful idea.

But we may go further. Not only must the argument demonstrate that God can be conceived coherently, it must also demonstrate that this conceivability is the only form of possibility required to guarantee real necessary existence. We have argued that in the case of a necessarily-existing being, to be possible and to be are the same. Granted the possibility, the actuality must follow. But the question is: precisely what *sort* of possibility will suffice to guarantee actual existence? In an argument which claims to deduce the real ontological existence of God, it would seem that nothing short of a demonstration of the *real* ontological potentiality of his existence will do. But does the *logical* possibility (i.e., conceivability) of that existence guarantee its *ontological* possibility--and hence its actuality? The argument must demonstrate an affirmative answer to this question. The proof must justify what Hartshorne calls its "doctrinal premise that meanings are logically possible only because referents are ontologically possible or actual."[14]

In short, two features of the proof merit special attention. One is that the argument assumes that perfection is a meaningful idea, and the other is that this subjective or epistemological or logical possibility is taken as sufficient evidence for the disjunction: real existence or real potency of existence. The fate of the argument hinges on the plausibility of these two points.

Consequently, there are two chief ways to challenge the argument. One is to hold, with the positivists, that the idea of God cannot be rendered coherent or intelligible. The other is to contend that what the argument requires--namely, the *real* possibility of the divine existence--is not proved by the mere *logical* possibility, or conceivability, of that existence. Or, in general, logical or linguistic modalities (necessity and possibility) do not necessarily correspond to real or ontological modalities. This would seem to be the sort of challenge that, for example, Kant was raising when he wrote:

> A concept is always possible if it is not self-contradictory. This is the logical criterion of possibility,...But it may none the less be an

> empty concept, unless the objective reality of the
> synthesis through which the concept is generated
> has been specifically proved; and such proof...
> rests on principles of possible experience, and
> not on the principle of analysis (the law of con-
> tradiction). *This is a warning against arguing*
> *directly from the logical possibility of concepts*
> *to the real possibility of things.*[15]

The first, or positivist, objection takes aim at Hartshorne's
theory of divinity, or theistic conceptuality, and the second,
or Kantian objection, at his theory of modality.

4. A Statement of the Thesis

According to the thesis that I am proposing, not only does
Hartshorne present a convincing case vis-à-vis both the positivist and the classical theist on the question of the conceivability of God, he also provides the principles for sound
arguments against those who hold to the radical disconnectedness of logical and ontological modalities. Furthermore, *the*
resources for both sets of arguments are to be found in exactly
the same place, namely, Hartshorne's metaphysics of temporal
possibility. Thus Hartshorne writes that "only a concretely
temporalistic theology can rightfully employ the Argument" (AD,
193, italics added), and he issues the challenge that "in order
to reject this proof one must construct a theory of possibility
which would not be required for ordinary purposes" (MVG, 301).

I turn now to an investigation of Hartshorne's metaphysics
of temporal possibility.

CHAPTER I

[1]Charles Hartshorne, *The Logic of Perfection* (LaSalle, IL: Open Court, 1962), pp. 50-51.

[2]The clause in parentheses does not appear in *The Logic of Perfection*, but has been added to all subsequent references to the proof at Hartshorne's request.

[3]In Chapter II, section 1.2, I distinguish between conditional and unconditional necessary truths, and between existential and non-existential necessary truths. In terms of that discussion, the "necessarily true" here should be taken as meaning *unconditionally* necessarily true. However, I see no reason why Becker's Rule would not cover the other types of necessary truth as well. Thus, for example, it is necessary (meaning, unconditionally necessary) that a conditionally necessary truth is conditionally necessary. An instance of a conditionally necessary truth is: 2 apples + 2 apples = 4 apples. This statement is necessarily true in every possible world in which there are apples. Thus, Becker's Rule says: it is true in *every* possible world that the proposition "2 apples + 2 apples = 4 apples" is necessarily true in every possible world in which there are apples. See Chapter II for further discussion of this point.

[4]R. L. Purtill, "Hartshorne's Modal Proof," *The Journal of Philosophy* 63/14 (July 14, 1966) 397-409. See also R. L. Purtill, *Logic for Philosophers* (New York: Harper & Row, 1971), pp. 256-60. Derivation of the theorem $(p \to \Box p) \supset (\Diamond p \to p)$ is as follows ("Hartshorne's Modal Proof," p. 398; *Logic for Philosophers*, pp. 256-57):

1. $\Box p \to p$		principles of modal logic
2. $\Diamond p \to \Box \Diamond p$		
3. $(p \to q) \to (\Box \sim q \to \Box \sim p)$		
4. $\sim \Box \sim p \to \Box \sim \Box \sim p$	(from 2 and the definition of $\Diamond p$)
5. $\sim \Box p \to \Box \sim \Box p$	(from 4 by substitution of $\sim p$ for p, and double negation)
6. $(p \to \Box p) \to (\Box \sim \Box p \to \Box \sim p)$	(from 3 by substitution of $\Box p$ for q)
*7. $p \to \Box p$	(Assumption for conditional proof)
*8. $\Box \sim \Box p \to \Box \sim p$	(7, 6, Modus ponens)
*9. $\sim \Box p \to \Box \sim p$	(5, 8, Hypothetical syllogism)
*10. $\sim \Box \sim p \to \Box p$	(9, Contraposition, Double negation)
*11. $\Diamond p \to \Box p$	(10 and definition of $\Diamond p$)
*12. $\Diamond p \to p$	(11, 1, Hypothetical syllogism)
13. $(p \to \Box p) \supset (\Diamond p \to p)$	(7-12, Conditional Proof)

[5]J. N. Findlay, "Reflections on Necessary Existence," in *Process and Divinity*, ed. William L. Reese and Eugene Freeman (LaSalle, IL: Open Court, 1964), pp. 521-22.

[6]*St. Anselm: Basic Writings*, trans. S. N. Deane, 2nd ed. (LaSalle: IL: Open Court, 1968), p. 8.

[7]*Inter alia*, cf. *Anselm's Discovery*, pp. 33-36 and p. 280; Hartshorne, *The Logic of Perfection*, p. 52.

[8]For precisely this reason some of the statements made by the "death of God" theologians and by the eschatological theologians must be regarded as inaccurate. That "God is dead" is, for example, a violation of the interior logic of the theistic concept, and is, strictly speaking, a misuse of the term "God." Necessary existence cannot be switched on and off. Likewise, Wolfhart Pannenberg's statement that "in a restricted but important sense, God does not yet exist...God's being is still in the process of coming to be" (*Theology and the Kingdom of God* [Philadelphia: Westminster Press, 1969], p. 56) is logically incorrect if it is taken as applying to the divine *existence* rather than to the divine *actuality*. See Chapter III, section 4, and Chapter IV, section 3.5.2, for discussion of the existence-actuality distinction.

[9]The connection between "Perfection" and necessary existence will be discussed further in Chapter III.

[10]Alvin Plantinga, *God, Freedom and Evil* (New York: Harper Torchbooks, 1974), p. 108.

[11]Hartshorne, "Formal Validity and Real Significance," p. 233.

[12]J. N. Findlay, "Can God's Existence be Disproved?" in *New Essays in Philosophical Theology*, ed. Antony Flew and Alasdair MacIntyre (New York: Macmillan, 1955), pp. 47-56.

[13]This simplified version of Hartshorne's proof comes from Purtill, "Hartshorne's Modal Proof," pp. 397-409. See also Purtill, *Logic for Philosophers*, p. 257.

[14]Hartshorne, "Formal Validity and Real Significance," p. 226.

[15]Immanuel Kant, *Critique of Pure Reason*, trans. Norman Kemp Smith (New York: Macmillan, 1970), p. 503n. Italics added.

CHAPTER II

THE METAPHYSICS OF TEMPORAL POSSIBILITY

In this chapter I want to examine closely what I consider
to be the key issue involved in Hartshorne's ontological argument, namely, his theory of temporal possibility. Metaphysical
potentiality is, for Hartshorne, to be interpreted wholly in
terms of *temporal* reality. He writes, for example, that "possibility has a natural basis in the character of what exists,
since to that character belongs an indeterminateness as to
future alternatives."[1] Before investigating this theory of
temporal possibility, however, it will be helpful to discuss
briefly, first, Hartshorne's understanding of what metaphysics
is; second, the two central tenets of his metaphysical system;
and, third, the three recurring principles that form the logical frame of that system. These preliminary observations will
help to guide us through an examination of the theory of possibility.

1. Hartshorne's Understanding of Metaphysics

In many ways and in many places, Hartshorne has proposed,
explained and defended his understanding of metaphysics as an
integral and independent form of inquiry. Indeed, an entire
essay could be written concerning Hartshorne's explication of
and arguments for the metaphysical task. In the second chapter
of *Creative Synthesis*--to cite only one example--he offers and
discusses no fewer than eleven definitions of metaphysics. Our
purpose here is to grasp what Hartshorne *means* by metaphysics
and to isolate the unique logical features of metaphysical assertions.

We may begin by saying that metaphysics, for Hartshorne,
is the search for the most general truths about the universe:
"The philosopher is seeking principles so general, so basic,
that they are no longer special cases to be explained by more
general principles, but are themselves the most general of
ideas" (RSP, 29). Or, as Whitehead put the point, the

philosopher is seeking principles which are so ultimate that "we never catch the actual world taking a holiday from their sway."[2]

How might we recognize these most general or ultimate truths? In what is perhaps his most basic statement on the subject, Hartshorne writes that metaphysics is best understood as "the search for unconditionally necessary truths about existence" (CS, 24). The peculiar characteristics of metaphysical truth, then, are: (1) that it is *necessary* truth, and (2) that it is *unconditionally* necessary, and therefore *existential*, truth.

1.1 *Metaphysical Truth is Necessary Truth*

Membership in the class of necessary truths distinguishes metaphysical assertions from all contingent, factual, empirical truths. "Contingent," "factual," and "empirical" are here used synonymously to refer to those assertions which conflict with some conceivable state of affairs (CS, 20). For example, "the pen is on the desk" conflicts with the conceivable state of affairs, "the pen is not on the desk." Factual statements are thus *partially* restrictive of existential possibilities (CS, 159). Most of our ordinary everyday assertions have this contingent, factual, empirical character. Necessary truths, on the other hand, are distinguished by their complete lack of conflict with any conceivable state of affairs. "All triangles have exactly three sides," for example, conflicts with no genuine possibility. Statements of this sort are *completely nonrestrictive* of existential possibilities (CS, 159). Necessary truths are thus all *a priori* in the sense that they contradict no conceivable observation (CS, 19).

The distinction between necessary (or *a priori*) and empirical (or factual) may be illustrated through a discussion of the falsification principle. It has been held, for example by Antony Flew,[3] that every meaningful assertion denies something, namely, its own negation. Symbolically, $p = \sim\sim p$. This is indeed correct. "The pen is on the desk" denies that "the pen is not on the desk"; "all triangles have exactly three sides"

denies that "some triangles do not have exactly three sides."
From this principle, however, Flew would have us conclude that
therefore every meaningful assertion must be capable of being
falsified. "Falsified" here means that what the assertion
denies ($\sim p$) could, conceivably at least, be exemplified or be
observed or be shown to exist.[4] For example, "the pen is on
the floor" is a conceivable and even demonstrable state of affairs that would serve to falsify "the pen is on the desk."
Likewise, it seems that "there are some four-sided triangles"
would serve to falsify "all triangles have exactly three sides."
But is the assertion, "some triangles have four sides," a conceivable or possible state of affairs? Given the meaning of
"triangle" and "four-sided," obviously not. The notion of a
"four-sided triangle" is as self-contradictory and impossible
as that of a "round square." In other words, while "the pen is
on the desk" both denies its own negation and can be falsified,
"all triangles have exactly three sides" denies its negation,
but cannot be falsified. All meaningful assertions deny their
negations, but not all meaningful assertions can be falsified.

Why is it that some meaningful assertions can be falsified, while others cannot? The answer is that some meaningful
assertions (i.e., the empirical ones) deny or exclude *significant* alternatives, alternatives that could be, under certain
circumstances, realized or illustrated. Other meaningful assertions (i.e., the necessary ones), however, deny or exclude
only nonsensical or impossible alternatives. And what is impossible can, for that very reason, never be shown to exist.
The denial of necessary truths can be verbal only.

To summarize: all empirical assertions are contingent by
virtue of their falsifiability; all necessary assertions, on
the other hand, share the common trait of immunity to falsification.

1.2 *Metaphysical Truths are Unconditional and so Existential*

Thus far we have argued that metaphysical assertions belong
to the class of necessary truths, and that necessary truths are
distinguished (from empirical truths) by their immunity to falsification. But not all necessary truths are metaphysical, and

here we must be very careful to specify *exactly* the marks of
metaphysical truth. Metaphysical truths, as Hartshorne's definition above indicates, are not only necessary truths, they are
unconditionally necessary as well, and therefore *existential*.

Following G. H. von Wright, Hartshorne distinguishes *conditionally* necessary truths from *unconditionally* necessary
truths (LP, 53). A conditionally necessary truth is one which
obtains upon certain conditions: necessity assuming p, or
necessity assuming not-p. "2 apples + 2 apples = 4 apples" is
a conditionally necessary truth, for its necessity depends upon
the (conditional) existence of apples. Or, put another way,
"2 apples + 2 apples = 4 apples" is not true in all possible
worlds, but only in those possible worlds in which there are
apples. Unconditional or absolute necessary truths, on the
other hand, are those which obtain upon tautological conditions:
necessity given p or not-p. Or, in effect (since p or not-p is
always the case), unconditionally necessary truths depend upon
no conditions whatsoever. "2 + 2 = 4" is an example.

Another distinction Hartshorne draws is that between
necessary statements which are *non-existential* and necessary
statements which are *existential* (that this is not exactly the
same distinction as conditional-unconditional will be shown
below). At least once Hartshorne has used the distinction between existential and non-existential necessity to describe the
difference between metaphysical and mathematical truth:

> Metaphysics, as I view it, studies non-restrictive
> existential affirmations. It differs from mathema-
> tics, which also studies non-restrictive statements,
> in that mathematical statements are non-existential.
> As usually interpreted they affirm, not that some-
> thing with a certain character exists, but that, if
> it did, such and such would also be the case. Thus
> they affirm relations between conceivable states of
> affairs, without affirming any such state to be ac-
> tualized. Mathematics explores possibilities; meta-
> physics tries to express what *all* possibilities of
> existence have in common. (CS, 162)

In other places, however, Hartshorne qualifies this distinction
between metaphysical and mathematical, as, for example, when he
suggests in *The Logic of Perfection* that arithmetical truth,
such as 2 + 2 = 4, may be metaphysical also (284). The proper

statement of Hartshorne's position, then, would seem to be this: *some* mathematical (and logical) truths are non-existential, while *others* are existential (and so metaphysical). How can we tell the difference? By determining if the possible worlds explored are *all* possible worlds, or *some* only. If some only are investigated, then the mathematical-logical truth is not metaphysical; if all are explored, then the truth is also metaphysical. At any rate, the distinction between necessary existential truth and necessary non-existential truth should be clear, even if Hartshorne is not always clear as to how *that* distinction applies to the distinction between metaphysical and mathematical-logical. Necessary existential truths are those truths which are necessarily true at least in this world; necessary non-existential truths are those truths which are necessarily true in *other* possible worlds, but not in this one.

(This seems to present a puzzle: how can something be necessarily true in this world, and yet not true at all in another possible world? Likewise, how can something be necessarily true in another possible world, and yet not true at all in this world? Or, to put the question yet a third way, how are such necessary truths different from contingent truths? The answer is this: something which is necessarily true in some world(s), but not all, must be only a *conditionally* necessary truth: it is necessarily true in any world in which certain conditions (which are themselves contingent) obtain. Thus the difference between conditionally necessary truths and contingent truths is this: the former are truths which are *necessary*, given certain conditions; the latter are truths which are only *contingently* true (or contingently false) in any possible world, or upon any conditions. "2 apples + 2 apples = 4 apples" is necessarily true in any possible world in which there are apples. "That there are apples," however, is only contingently true (or false) in any possible world. By the very meaning of "apple," this proposition could never be necessary. Or, to put the difference another way: contingent truths are those which are true in some possible worlds and *false in other possible worlds*; conditionally necessary truths are those which are necessarily true in some possible worlds and *false in no possible worlds.* For example, "2 zorks + 2 zorks = 4 zorks" is not exactly true in this world, because there are no "zorks"; but neither is it exactly false, because no case of "2 zorks + 2 zorks ≠ 4 zorks" can even be conceived. If we assign the value +1 to true statements, and -1 to false statements, we should say that "2 zorks + 2 zorks = 4 zorks" has zero truth value in this world.)

Combining the distinction between conditional and unconditional with the distinction between existential and non-existential, then, we arrive at a formal classification of four kinds of necessary truth, only one of which is genuinely metaphysical. Necessary truths may be: (1) conditional and existential, (2) conditional and non-existential, (3) unconditional and existential, or (4) unconditional and non-existential. Discussion of each type will clarify *exactly* what Hartshorne means by metaphysical truth.

There can be no examples of a necessary truth which is both unconditional and non-existential. A truth which depends upon no conditions whatsoever will be true in *all* possible worlds, and therefore in the actual one as well, and so will be existential. Classification (4) is therefore a verbal classification only.

Can there be necessary truths which are conditional and non-existential (2)? Obviously there can be. Many systems of mathematical-logical truth are wholly consistent deductions from postulates that do not reflect any *actual* state of affairs. Some schemes of non-Euclidean geometry, for instance, are not derived from the laws of actual physical space. Such geometrical truths are necessary, but non-existential. They tell us, not what is necessarily the case in this world, but what would necessarily be the case in another possible world with such-and-such laws. They are also only conditionally necessary, that is, necessary, assuming certain postulates which are not *themselves* necessary.

Can there be necessary truths which are conditional and existential (1)? Certainly anything which is necessary, *given* this actual state of the universe, would seem to fit this classification. In several places Hartshorne suggests that

many of the physical laws of the universe are instances of conditionally necessary existential truth.[5] Is the speed of light,
for example, a necessary constant in *any* conceivable universe
(and so unconditionally necessary) or only in *this* (and perhaps
some other) phase or epoch of world process (and so, only conditionally, although existentially, necessary)? The same could
be asked about the laws of acceleration, gravity, the conversion
of mass into energy, and so forth. I do not try to resolve
these matters here; they can be decided, if at all, only by
those who are highly skilled both in theoretical physics and in
metaphysics. But, if the speed of light, for example, could
genuinely and conceivably have been different, then it is an
example of a conditional and existential necessary truth. That
is the point.

At any rate, the difficulty of deciding such cases as (1)
and (2) should not obscure the essentially clear meaning of
necessary truths which are unconditional and so existential (3).
These are the properly *metaphysical* truths. (For the present,
I am concerned merely with the characteristics of such truth,
and I postpone for a moment the question of whether there are
instances of metaphysical truth.)

We may now summarize the unique status of metaphysical
truths. Being *necessary*, metaphysical truths could not be falsified, and this distinguishes them from all empirical or factual truths. While empirical truths are true in some possible
worlds and false in other possible worlds, metaphysical truths,
as necessary, cannot be false in any possible world. Being *unconditional*, metaphysical truths are true in *all* possible
worlds, and this distinguishes them from conditional necessary
truths. Being *existential*, metaphysical truths are illustrated
in the actual world, and this distinguishes them from non-
existential necessary truths.

An important consequence follows from this discussion.
All necessary non-existential truths and all conditionally
necessary truths are true in all possible worlds *in which the
requisite conditions obtain*. All metaphysical (unconditionally
necessary, and therefore existential) truths, on the other hand,
are true in all possible worlds *simpliciter*. The generic

criterion for necessary truth as such, therefore, is *falsity in no possible world*; and the specific criterion for metaphysical truth is *truth in all possible worlds*.

Being necessary *and* unconditional *and* existential, therefore, metaphysical truths are not only immune to falsification by anything that is so much as even conceivable, they are, in addition, *bound* to be verified by every actual or possible state of affairs. This distinguishes metaphysical truth from *all* other kinds of truth, empirical and necessary. We may thus recognize a genuine metaphysical truth in this way: it will reflect an idea which is *actually* known to be true and which could not even *possibly* not be true.

An implication of the foregoing, directly relevant to this thesis, should be noted here. Since, as Hartshorne argues, the assertion, "Necessarily, God exists," is a metaphysical assertion, it is, if true, unconditionally true as well (LP, 53). This means that we are *not* free to argue that it is "merely" logically true, where the "merely" is taken to indicate necessary truth of the conditional or the non-existential kind. If "God exists" is necessarily true, it is true upon no conditions whatsoever, and so it is true not only in *some* possible worlds, but in *every* possible world, including, therefore, the actual world. "Thus if God logically could be necessary He must be, since no contingent conditions can be relevant" (LP, 53). (See below, Chapter IV, section 2, for further discussion of this point.) All metaphysical truths have this character.

1.3 *An Example of Metaphysical Truth*

We have been isolating the unique marks of metaphysical truth: such truth is necessary and unconditional and (therefore) existential. Now we must face an obvious and important question: *are* there indeed instances of such truth?[6]

Hartshorne's prime candidate for metaphysical truth is the assertion, "something exists." This proposition indeed fulfills all the requirements of metaphysical truth. In the first place, "something exists" is not even conceivably falsifiable, and so is a *necessary* truth. "Something exists" denies that nothing exists, and "nothing exists" is a literally inconceivable and nonsensical proposition. In order to illustrate or verify "nothing exists," one thing at least would have to exist, namely, the being which is illustrating or verifying. And if one thing exists, something exists.

In the second place, therefore, literally everything which does or has or could exist illustrates or verifies "something exists." Not only is the proposition universally immune to falsification, it is also universally verifiable by whatever is so much as even possible. "Something exists" is therefore *unconditionally* necessary.

In the third place, the proposition has obvious application to the actual world (this follows, of course, from the truth that it is unconditionally necessary). "Something exists" is thus *existential* as well.

Unless and until it can be shown that "something exists" is neither meaningful nor unconditionally necessary nor existential, Hartshorne's case for metaphysics would seem to be entirely plausible. That there are, in addition, other metaphysical truths will be argued below.[7] Metaphysics is the discipline which searches for those general truths about existence which are unconditionally necessary. The point of this study is to support Hartshorne's contention that "God exists" is one such truth.

2. Two Central Metaphysical Doctrines

Given this understanding of the formal character of metaphysical inquiry, we may turn now to questions of content. What, materially speaking, is distinctive about Hartshorne's metaphysics? Hartshorne's characterization of Whitehead's philosophy as "a philosophy which makes process and relativity the inclusive conceptions, and which makes experience as such the universal form of reality" (WP, 119) stands as an excellent summary analysis of Hartshorne's own metaphysics. The summary involves two central points: (1) that "becoming" or "relativity" or "process" or "creativity" is the ultimate metaphysical *principle*, and (2) that experiences are the final metaphysical *facts*. I suggest that the two propositions, "necessarily, experience occurs" and "necessarily, creative synthesis occurs,"

distinguish Hartshorne's process philosophy from all philosophies of being and metaphysics of substance. Let us now examine these two doctrines closely.

2.1 *Necessarily, Experience Occurs: The Final Metaphysical Facts*

Whitehead wrote that "the final problem [in speculative
philosophy] is to conceive a complete fact."[8] By a "complete
fact" Whitehead meant that which exists in and of itself, or
that which is possessed of full existence; in short, the ultimate "building blocks" or the final metaphysical units of
reality. Plato held these complete facts to be the Forms,
Aristotle spoke of substances or individual essences, and Leibniz called them monads.

The process philosophies of Whitehead and Hartshorne characterize the final metaphysical facts as "actual entities."[9]
This technical term is carefully chosen. "Entity" is to be
understood as "event" or "occasion" in distinction to "thing"
or "substance," and it expresses Hartshorne's doctrine that
entities, not substances, are the ultimate metaphysical facts.
Strictly speaking, entities do not *exist*; things or substances
--such as persons, trees, houses--exist, whereas entities *occur*
or are actual. The "actual" in "actual entity," then, expresses
"the doctrine that actuality is the basic concept in this philosophy, not existence" (WP, 120). Thus, one of the distinguishing factors of Hartshorne's metaphysics is that actual entities, not existing substances, are taken to be metaphysically
ultimate.

An example will illustrate the distinction between actual
entities and existing substances. Consider the statement, "I
exist." This is, for Hartshorne, a derivative and abstract
truth for two reasons: (1) The "I" refers to a particular substance, a relatively unchanging and identical subject. In this
sense I am the same person at age thirty that I was at age five
and will be at age sixty. But in another sense I am obviously
different from day to day. Yesterday, for example, I was sick;
today I am well. Schooling has changed my knowledge; growth
has changed my appearance, etc. How are we to reconcile these

twin truths that I am both the *same* person from day to day, and
yet also a changing, and so different, person? The answer, for
Hartshorne, lies in the distinction between substance and event
(or actuality): substances are abstract identities, events are
the differing states. I am the same in my identity, but different in my actual states. Now, what changes (the concrete
states) can contain an abstract element of changelessness (substantial identity); but not *vice versa*. Thus we may reconcile
the two truths of changelessness and change in our case simply
by noting that substantial identity is an abstraction from
successive states, each of which becomes but does not change.

Hartshorne concludes from this line of reasoning that entities, as states or events, are metaphysically more fundamental than substances. This is to say that substances are in
events, not the other way, because substances are *abstractions*
from events. "The notion of substance that it is an identical
entity containing successive accidental properties is an absurdity, a misleading way of describing an individual enduring
through change. The successive states are not 'in' the identical entity but rather it is in them" (CS, 20). My identity,
for example, is a feature abstracted from the concrete states
in which I exist. "Identity is a somewhat abstract view of a
personal history" (WP, 181). I shall have more to say about
this distinction between actual entities and individual substances in Chapter IV when I discuss the substance versus the
genetic or event theory of identity.[10] For the present I want
only to point out that in Hartshorne's philosophy the primacy
of events over substances means that "the concrete units of
reality are not individual persons or things but events or
states" (WP, 180).

(2) Likewise, the "exist" in "I exist" is an abstraction
from something more fundamental. Existence refers to the truth
that a substance is; actuality refers to *how* or in what precise
state the individual substance exists. For example, at this
moment I am writing; the relatively concrete act of writing
thus defines the particular *how* of my existence at this precise
moment, and the bare truth that I exist is, by comparison, abstract. Existence is an abstraction from a set or series of

actual states. *That* I exist is a truth which may be exemplified in many different actual states: sleeping, playing, work-
ing, etc. Existence means *somehow* actualized. Thus, in exactly the same way that events include, and so are more basic
than, substances, so actuality includes, and hence is more
basic than, existence.

What, exactly, are actual entities? Hartshorne uses the
phrase, "occasions of experience," to characterize them. This
means that, for Hartshorne, the final metaphysical units of
reality are discrete "drops" of experience, and he suggests
that in human experience there may be perhaps twenty such "experient occasions" each second, while on the atomic level there
may be unit-becomings thousands or millions of times shorter
than a twentieth of a second. Metaphysically speaking, then,
Hartshorne conceives of a panpsychic universe consisting of
myriads of nearly instantaneous acts of experience, each dependent on its predecessors.

Why does Hartshorne conceive of actual entities as acts of
experience? The answer lies in Hartshorne's "turn to the subject." It was Descartes who introduced into philosophical
method the principle that "those substances which are
the subjects enjoying conscious experiences, provide the primary data for philosophy, namely, themselves as in the enjoyment of such experience."[11] Thus, what deserves primary philosophical attention is not a perceived substance qualified by
an accidental state (the stone, for example, qualified by grey),
but rather my *experience* of, or my perception of, or my subjective enjoyment of the grey stone. If there is any philosophically neutral starting point, it is surely this: my subjective
experience-of. All else is less definitely given in its status
and nature. This, then, is the famous "turn to the subject"
which entered western thought through Descartes.

To be completely faithful to Descartes' insight, however,
we need to balance his discovery on the side of the subject
with an objectivist principle as to the datum of experience.
In other words, if the subjective enjoyment of experience is
the *ultimate* metaphysical fact, then *what* a subject experiences
(the object) is *itself* a subject enjoying experience. What

else can "ultimate" mean? This is the *Reformed* Subjectivist
Principle of process philosophy: "the whole universe consists
of elements disclosed in the analysis of the experiences of
subjects" (Whitehead).[12] Or, in Hartshorne's words, "to be a
subject of experience is to have other subjects as objects,
forming a world system of such subjects" (CS, 114). In short,
Hartshorne's description of the final metaphysical units as
occasions of experience derives from the argument that what the
turn to the subject discloses as metaphysically *ultimate* is the
subjective enjoyment of experience.

A common objection to Hartshorne's philosophy is that it
is simply silly to say that stones and trees and houses "experience." This objection betrays a gross misunderstanding of
Hartshorne's position; nowhere, for example, does he say that
trees "experience." What he argues, rather, is that the notion
of substance (tree or stone or chair or what have you) is an
abstraction from more basic metaphysical realities (namely,
"actual entities"), and that when these actual entities (from
which the substances are derived) are analyzed, *they* have the
character of acts of experience.

This leads to a second common objection, namely that
Hartshorne's philosophy is too exclusively ego-centric or
anthropomorphic. Why should all reality have the experiencing
character of *human* reality? This, too, is a misunderstanding
of Hartshorne's philosophy. In the phrase, "occasions of experience," "experience" is used in a technical metaphysical
sense, and should not be identified with *human* experience.[13]
In much the same way that traditional philosophies spoke of
human and non-human *substances*, Hartshorne speaks of human and
non-human *experiences*, the difference being that experiences
are here taken to be more fundamental than substances.

To be sure, human experience is the *paradigm* for metaphysical generalization, because it is a highly refined grade
or level of experience, and the form of experience immediately
available for philosophical investigation. It is not, however,
the *whole* of experience, because, to state the Reformed Subjectivist Principle once again, *whatever* a human subject experiences is itself a subject enjoying experiences. "Experience

is never merely of some insentient 'object,' but is always experience of others' experience" (WP, 168).

In other words, human experience contains both those distinguishing features (such as explicit consciousness) which
make it specifically *human* experience) *and* those more fundamental features which are constitutive of all experience,
simply as such. It is these fundamental features which characterize all actual entities as occasions of experience. For
example, one fundamental feature of all experience is related-
ness, or better, sociality: experience is always experience-of.
There can be no such thing as a completely isolated experience,
wholly unrelated to anything else. The social structure of
experience refers to the truth that all experience consists of
the direct apprehension of other experiences. "Experience must
have stimuli; there must be objects of experience, data which
are already there, ready to be experienced. Yet in this philosophy there is nothing in the world but creative experience.
What, then, are the objects that are there to be experienced?
Simply, previous cases of experience!" (CS, 7). Memory is the
clearest example of this principle of experience of experience.
When I remember an event, the Kennedy assassination, for example, I am experiencing precisely my previous experience.

The sociality of all acts of experiencing points in two
directions. On the one hand, it refers to the fact that every
experience depends on previous experiences for its own occurrence. Whitehead used the term "prehension" to stress this
element of pure givenness in an act of experience, experience
as the having of an object. In Hartshorne's words, "the con-
straint of the past upon the present is simply that an experience cannot generate its own data, but must find them in what
has already occurred" (CS, 117). This is Whitehead's doctrine
of "causal efficacy" or conformation: the present occasion of
experience is just a certain way of prehending its past.
"Causal efficacy is thus not a merely mysterious link between
earlier and later; it is the fairly obvious truth that there
cannot be prehension of x without x, and since prehension cannot be creative of its antecedent objects, they must be fur-
nished to it by the actual past" (WP, 126).

On the other hand, the sociality of experience refers to the truth that every experience is destined to become a datum prehended by some later experience. This is Whitehead's doctrine of "objective immortality." What is objectified and handed over to the future as datum is precisely what makes an experience *this* unique experience, namely, the subjective enjoyment or the novel synthesis of other experiences. Whitehead used the metaphor of "perishing" to describe this objectification of the subjective enjoyment of an act of experience for other, future, experiences. Perishing refers to the truth that, in the transition from present to past, the subjective experiencing of an actual entity becomes objectified as a datum that is experienced. "To perish, in this technical sense, is not to be 'annihilated,' or even changed into a diminished reality;... The entity completes its decision...and the finished entity is then accepted by the next synthesis as a datum. To perish and to become objectifiable by new entities are the same" (WP, 127).[14] In short, experient occasions have an irreducibly social character: they arise out of the prehension of previous experiences, and in turn become data for prehension by subsequent occasions. Causal efficacy and objective immortality are thus reverse readings of the same insight that experience is always experience of other experience.

To the metaphysical proposition, "necessarily, something exists," we may thus add the equally general truth, "necessarily, experience occurs." Note that the proposition does not say that *human* experience necessarily occurs,[15] but rather that "there are experiences of some kind" is an unconditionally necessary truth. Why is the proposition unconditionally necessary? In the first place, it is not conceivably falsifiable. What would "experience does not occur" mean, and how would it be known, "since anything, if it comes to be known, must exhibit its character in some experience" (CS, 164)? The nonoccurrence of experience is literally unknowable or inconceivable, from which Hartshorne rightly concludes that if the statement "experience occurs" is existentially restrictive, there is no way to ascertain this. It follows that there is no possible world in which "experience occurs" could not be known

to be true. Finally, "experience occurs" has obvious application to this world; our own experience occurs, for example.
"Experience occurs" thus fulfills the requirements of metaphysical necessity: "an idea actually known to be true in some
cases, but not even potentially known to be false in any *conceivable* case, is for all purposes an ultimate idea" (RSP, 33).

To summarize: one of the two central features of Hartshorne's philosophy is that it takes the final metaphysical
facts to be, not existing substances (these are not, however,
unreal; rather, they are abstractions), but the occurrences of
actual entities, which are occasions of experience. This doctrine is the result of an exploitation of Descartes' insight
that the subjective enjoyment of experience is the Archimedean
truth for metaphysical generalization. "Neo-classicism takes a
momentary experience as the model or paradigm of concrete reality" (CS, 128). Being metaphysically ultimate, these actual
occasions constitute *all* reality, human, sub-human, and supra-
human (if there be such). The common character of these experient occasions is sociality, a doctrine succinctly stated in
the title of one of Hartshorne's books, *Reality as Social Process*. This entire discussion is implicit in the metaphysical
proposition: Necessarily, experience occurs.

2.2 *Necessarily, Creative Synthesis Occurs: the Ultimate
      Metaphysical Principle*

In Hartshorne's philosophy, the ultimate metaphysical
principle is simply that principle which expresses the character of all the final metaphysical facts; it is the most general
and most abstract feature shared by all occasions of experience.
As we argued above, the final metaphysical facts, as experient
occasions, are intrinsically social: every experience is always
experience of other experiences. Thus the basic character of
all actual entities is that they arise out of previous experiences and in turn become data for further experiences. This is
the principle of creative synthesis, or process. In Whitehead's words: "The ultimate metaphysical principle is the advance from disjunction to conjunction, creating a novel entity
other than the entities given in disjunction....The many become
one, and are increased by one."[16]

This principle of creative synthesis explains both permanence and novelty in the universe. Experience of experience is
a synthesis precisely of *antecedent* data--and this accounts for
order, stability and permanence. But the act of synthesis is
also a holding together of the data in a *new* unity--and this
accounts for novelty. "The new whole is thus in some degree
unpredictable and 'emergent'" (CS, 165).

Creative synthesis denies absolute determinism as well as
absolute indeterminism, both of which, Hartshorne argues, are
impossible states of affairs. Absolute determinism, the denial
of *all* novelty in the universe, is falsified by every new and
unpredictable state of affairs. I am genuinely free to finish
this essay or not to finish it. Determinism, therefore, cannot
be absolute. On the other hand, absolute indeterminism, the
denial of all order, would be supreme chaos--and so would be
absolutely unknowable.[17] In short, what the principle of relative indeterminism (or, equally, relative determinism) denies
are not possible states of affairs, but only nonsensical states
of affairs. It follows that the proposition, "creative synthesis occurs," "has the complete flexibility characteristic of
non-restrictive or metaphysically valid ideas" (CS, 165).

(This principle of creative advance contains, in outline,
Hartshorne's entire theory of possibility, for process *means*
that "it is an inalienable aspect of the determinate actuality
of the world now that its next stage is not wholly determinate
but determinable in certain directions and to a determined ex-
tent."[18] Hartshorne's ultimate metaphysical principle says
that it is of the very character of actuality to include future
alternatives. It is thus an implication of creativity that
possibility is a property of existent things and not independent of all existence.)

Hartshorne's entire philosophy may be understood as the
systematic elucidation of this single point: that creative becoming, or process, is the ultimate principle of reality.
"Ultimate" here means both "all-inclusive" and "all-pervasive":
that which includes, as specializations, all other metaphysical
truths, and so cannot itself be explained in terms of anything
more general or more basic; and that which pervades all the

final metaphysical facts. Creativity is thus the metaphysical principle which explains all lesser principles: "Causality, substance, memory, perception, temporal succession, modality, are all but modulations of one principle of creative synthetic experiencing, feeding entirely upon its own prior products" (CS, 107). It is also the principle which must be exemplified by every concrete actuality:

> What makes it [creativity] metaphysical is just its absolute generality, by which is meant that any actual entity must exhibit it. Since what is not an actual entity is either, according to the system, a group of such entities, or an abstraction from one or more of them, everything whatever will in some fashion embody or manifest creativity. Not that one is to say that a river or a tree literally creates, but that when the river or tree is analyzed into the concrete singular components constituting its history, crea- tivity will characterize these components, i.e., the actual entities involved. (WP, 174)

Thus Hartshorne contends that the metaphysical ultimacy traditionally accorded to "being" is, in fact, a derivative-- and hence not an ultimate--feature of reality. The basic argu- ment is one of comprehensiveness: if we assume that being is the ultimate principle we generate antinomies when we attempt to explain how our experience of change and becoming can be de- rived from or explained in terms of this final truth. The static cannot contain or explain the dynamic. Becoming, on the other hand, may more plausibly be regarded as the ultimate category, because a developing whole can include an abstract feature of permanence or identity. "Whereas 'becoming' can be taken as inclusive without suppressing the contrast between it- self and being, 'being' taken as inclusive would destroy this contrast" (CS, 13).

Contained in this simple, central thesis is the whole in- terior logic of neoclassical metaphysics, which Hartshorne has articulated in three principles: (1) the Law of Polarity, (2) the Law of Inclusive Contrast, and (3) the distinction between concrete and abstract. A discussion of these logical princi- ples will assist us in interpreting Hartshorne's doctrine of possibility.

3. Logical Features of Hartshorne's Metaphysics

In the introduction to *Creative Synthesis* Hartshorne en-
dorses May Sinclair's statement that "logic is the backbone of
philosophy" (CS, xvii), and thus he writes that "the basic decisions are not as to metaphors, but as to logical structure.
What depends upon what, what includes what, what is necessary
to or contingent upon what?" (CS, 129). Indeed, one of the
most attractive features of Hartshorne's metaphysics is that it
exhibits and employs a clear, consistent, and identifiable
logical structure. Furthermore, it can be argued that this
logic is more comprehensive, more adequate to categories derived from experience, than the logic of classical metaphysics.[19] We may summarize the features which form the logical backbone of Hartshorne's system in three principles.

3.1 *The Law of Polarity*

Hartshorne contends that metaphysical categories always
come in pairs of ultimate contraries, such as being-becoming,
necessity-contingency, immutability-change, eternity-time,
cause-effect, absolute-relative, unity-variety, etc. "In every
experience, if it is sufficiently reflective, certain abstract
contrasts may be noted as somehow relevant, e.g., complex-
simple, effect-cause. These contrasts are the ultimate or
metaphysical contraries" (CS, 99). Adopting Morris Cohen's
"law of polarity,"[20] Hartshorne argues that these "ultimate
contraries are correlatives, mutually interdependent, so that
nothing real can be described by the wholly one-sided assertion
of simplicity, being, actuality, and the like, each in a 'pure'
form, devoid and independent of complexity, becoming, potentiality, and related contraries" (PSG, 2). The law of polarity
is thus a law of *di*polarity: metaphysical contraries are interdependent, so that neither term *means* in isolation. If either
term is real, the contrast--which includes both poles--is also
real.

3.2 *The Law of Inclusive Contrast*

To say that polarities are ultimate, however, is not to say that both poles are on an equal footing. "The ultimacy of dualities does not validate dualism" (CS, 90). It is one thing to say that being and becoming require one another for their meaning, and quite another to say that being-and-becoming is an ultimate metaphysical principle. According to the law of inclusive contrast, the relation between ultimate contraries is not one of conjunction, but one of inclusion: not a *and* b, but a *in* b. Thus, there is not being and becoming, but being in becoming, necessity in contingency, etc.

Furthermore, the relation of inclusion must be asymmetrical, which is to say that it can obtain in only one direction; for, while one term in each polarity can include the other without destroying the contrast between them, the converse relation would destroy the contrast. Consider the polarity, necessary-contingent. It must be contingency which includes necessity; for how could necessity in any way contain contingency, since the necessary is by definition wholly non-contingent? To consider our previous example: "2 apples + 2 apples = 4 apples" is a conditionally necessary truth which illustrates how contingent conditions (the existence of apples) may contain a necessary truth (2 + 2 = 4). "The concept expressing the total reality is the entire truth, not because the correlative contrary can be dismissed or negated, but because the referents of the latter are included in those of the former, while the converse inclusion does not obtain. Thus a basic asymmetry is involved" (CS, 100).

Logical analysis illustrates Hartshorne's point. Consider the following argument (LP, 184): (1) Conjunctive relationships, such as being and becoming, are symmetrical: there is no order or direction in a mere "and." (2) Symmetrical relations can be derived from asymmetrical ones, but not vice versa. Thus, to say that "x is equal to y" merely means that neither is greater than the other. On the other hand, "x is greater than y" cannot be derived from the mere denial of their symmetry. (3) Therefore, asymmetrical relations are ultimate, and symmetrical ones derivative. "The ultimate relations must then be non-symmetrical or directional" (LP, 184). "This pattern, symmetry within an overall asymmetry, we meet again and again. I see in it a paradigm for metaphysics. What we are to look for in basic concepts is comprehensive asymmetry or directional order embracing a subordinate aspect of symmetry" (CS, 210).

3.3 *The Concrete Inclusion of the Abstract*

It is helpful, in discussing the law of inclusive contrast, to recognize that one term in each contrast refers to *concrete* realities, the other to *abstract* dimensions of those concrete realities. "One pole is abstract and exclusive, the other concrete and inclusive" (CS, 269). Terms like "being," "necessity," "immutability," "eternity" are one and all abstract terms (Hartshorne names them "a terms," for "absolute"). "Becoming," "contingency," "change," "time," are all descriptions of concrete reality ("r terms," for "relative"). The concrete is fundamental, the abstract derivative. The concrete includes the abstract, and the abstract is real only as a dimension or generic feature of the concrete. We are to understand the principle of inclusive contrast on this model of the concrete inclusion of the abstract: being is an abstract feature of becoming, necessity is an abstract feature of a contingent whole, etc. Thus, for example, there is no contradiction in affirming that a man both *is* and *becomes*, for the assertions are made of different aspects of the man. He *is* (in his abstract identity) at thirty the same person as the boy of five, but he changes, and so is different, in every successive concrete state. And note, each concrete state includes the man's past history, which means, contains the abstract features of identity which run through all those states.

This distinction between concrete and abstract is so central to Hartshorne's philosophy that he can argue that "strictly speaking, there is but *one* metaphysical, innate or strictly universal and necessary idea or principle, concreteness (containing internally its own contrast to abstractness)" (CS, 32). And he can characterize metaphysics as "the unrestrictive or completely general theory of concreteness" (CS, 24).[21]

4. Hartshorne's Theory of Temporal Possibility

Given this preliminary study of Hartshorne's metaphysics--
its purpose, central tenets and logical features--we may turn
to an examination of his theory of temporal possibility.

Temporality and modality are central categories in a metaphysics of process. If metaphysics is the general theory of
concreteness, it is also "the theory of objective modality"
(CS, 24), because "the structure of time or becoming is inherent in concreteness (and in factual truth) as such, and...this
structure is modal" (CS, 29). Time expresses the very character of becoming: process is *temporal* process, it is the cease-
less advance of the present into the future and the preserva-
tion of the moments of this advance everlastingly in the past.
Modality is a central category, because temporality, and hence
process, has an irreducibly modal structure. Following Aristotle and Peirce, Hartshorne holds that time is objective modality and that modality is essentially temporal. Thus he
speaks interchangeably of "the temporal aspect of modality, or
the modal aspect of temporality" (AD, 145), and he argues that
"modal distinctions are ultimately coincident with temporal
ones" (CS, 61). This is to say, for example, that the modal
distinction between actuality, possibility and necessity is a
temporal distinction. Let us unpack both sides of Hartshorne's
thesis: (1) time is objective modality; (2) modality is essentially temporal.

4.1 *Time is Objective Modality*

Augustine posed an interesting puzzle: if to be real is to
be present, then how do we explain the past and the future?[22]
Are they simply unreal, or are they objectively real but subjectively hidden from view, or are they real in some sense different from what is real *now*? One answer to this question is
that time is *modal*, that is, that different modes of reality
are involved in temporality. We distinguish among past, present and future, and among memory, decision and anticipation.
These distinctions are modal distinctions. The past is the
realm of actuality. Memory is in principle (although not

always in fact) vivid, because when we remember, we prehend definite, determinate, fully concrete past actualities. The future is modally distinct from the past, because the future is the realm of indefinite, indeterminate and determinable possibilities. In anticipation we perceive only outlines, tendencies, probabilities--but never actualities. Anticipation is in principle vague, just because there are no future actualities to know.

What, then, is the present? Can we so refine the notion of past and future, or of actual and possible, that the present instant becomes a specious entity? This is Zeno's paradox applied to time. According to Hartshorne, the present is not, strictly speaking, either actual or possible. "'Actual' process is past process, rather than strictly present process... actuality is pastness, since presentness is a becoming actual rather than a being actual" (CS, 117-18). Both Whitehead and Hartshorne have argued that time is not--metaphysically speaking--infinitely divisible into phases of earlier and later. Rather, time advances in discrete pulses which are quanta of becoming.[23] These final "drops" are not temporally divisible because they are themselves the ultimate measure of time. Time is thus the relation *between* these final units: "being past is relative, meaning that some new present has the entity as its past" (WP, 166). Being future is also relative, for it is an extrapolation from what is present to what is possible, given this present.

It may seem troublesome that the present is not yet actual. But this is only to say that *becoming* actual is distinct from *being* actual. Whitehead's principle of relativity says that "the very 'being' of an entity is its availability for objectification" (WP, 166), so that "to be" and "to be objectified" are the same. But in order to be objectified, the actual entity must first complete its process of self-creative becoming and achieve a determinate satisfaction. "It first completes its process of becoming, and then it is objectified. There is nothing between" (WP, 165-66). Thus if a present entity--say E_1--were *as present* already actual (as opposed to becoming actual), it would be datum for other actual entities. But for

which other entities? Certainly not for future entities--there
are none such. Nor for past entities, for they have already
become actual. What then? Only for *strictly contemporary*
entities. But if these entities, as present, are also already
actual, they have already completed the process of self-
creation, and so by definition no longer prehend. Thus E_1 is
datum for no entity whatsoever, which is to say, it is not
actual at all. The same argument would apply to all other con-
temporaries: they would neither prehend nor be prehended, much
like the Leibnizian monads. Thus the doctrine that "the present is nascent, it is coming into being, rather than in being"
(CS, 109) entails the further doctrine that strict contemporar-
ies do not prehend one another.[24] Prehension is always of the
past. This is why Hartshorne holds that memory is the key to
perception.[25]

The immediate present, then, is composed of many contemporary and causally independent units of becoming, which are
the occasions of experience that we discussed above. This notion of irreducible units of experience explains how past and
future *are* real; for it designates the metaphysical locus of
actuality and possibility in the present. To be past and to be
prehended by, or inherited for, the present prehending experience are one and the same. "The pastness of an entity is the
same as its being objectified by successors" (WP, 165). The
relation of the past to the present is one of causal efficacy;
the past is *in* the present as objects are in the subjects which
prehend them, or as causes are in their effects. The relation
of the present to the future is one of teleological anticipation; the future is *in* the present as effects are in their
causes: the objectification of this present experience will
contribute to the experience which constitutes some (antecedently undetermined) future subject. The past is in the present
as ancestor; the future is in the present as descendant.

To say that time is *modal*, therefore, is to say that the
being of the past is modally different from the being of the
future. Time includes a retrospective or preservative mode of
being (actuality or pastness) and a prospective or creative
mode of being (possibility or futurity). "Modal distinctions

are ultimately coincident with temporal ones. The actual is the past, the possible is the future" (CS, 61).

To say that time is *objective* modality is to say that the distinction between past and future, or between actuality and possibility, is in *no* sense merely epistemological or only anthropomorphic. It is to deny that time is, from any point of view--even that of eternity or omniscience--a pure succession of actual events, as opposed to an irreversible, asymmetrical, cumulative process consisting in the actualization of possibility. The future is not merely subjectively possible; it is objectively as well as subjectively the realm of possibility. With Hartshorne I would agree that the burden of proof rests (and heavily) on those who would assert that the future is *objectively* other than the realm of possibility. The theory "that that which to us is future possesses objectively the same reality as that which to us is present or past...is a quite special and by no means self-evident doctrine about time" (MVG, 98).

An important consequence of the doctrine that time is objective modality is that we must reconceive both the meaning of eternity and the relation of time to eternity. Most emphatically, eternity cannot be understood as an a-temporal (meaning *extra*-temporal) order of being. *We have just argued that process is ultimate, that process is temporal, and that temporality is irreducibly modal.* An a-temporal conception of eternity would, in addition, violate the law of polarity. Time and eternity are metaphysical contraries, and so require one another for their meanings.

Hartshorne handles the question of eternity and time in exactly the same way that he deals with the relation of being to becoming. Which category is inclusive, and which is derivative; what includes or explains what? Obviously, eternity cannot include time, because the changeless cannot include the changing. "For if the parts of a whole become, so does the whole, and if the whole does not, certainly the parts do not. Change is sheer illusion if there is an immutable final totality of changes" (PSG, 93). The relation of inclusion must obtain in the other direction: it is time which includes eternity.

In Hartshorne's words, "eternity is a function of time" (CS, 29). This is a clear illustration of the law of inclusive contrast.

No doubt it will seem strange to think of eternity as somehow *within* time. But consider: if the essential meaning of temporality is the actualization of possibility, then to be "in time" simply means to be in possibilities that are actualized. Now, we can distinguish two ways of being in time: temporally and eternally. If an individual is in time temporally, its continued existence is ingredient in a *limited* number of possibilities that may or may not come to be actualized. Put the other way, the individual's existence is eventually excluded by some possibility that is actualized. Obviously, then, we may allow for the case of an individual's being in time eternally, if "to be eternal" means to be ingredient in *every* possibility, and thus to be incapable of non-actualization. The eternal is that which is common to all futures, or that which constitutes possibility as such, and so is bound to be actualized. Furthermore, that which is instantiated in the concrete actualization of every possibility can only be highly abstract--this is precisely why it can be illustrated by every concrete unit of temporal process.

We have, then, a rule, at once logical and metaphysical, which explains both the character of the concrete temporal whole and how that whole not only admits but requires an exception to that character in the form of a distinguishable abstract feature. "Either there must be a more truly universal Rule, which illustrates the lesser rules, and explains why they not only admit but demand an Exception, or else the idea of the Exception is against all logic" (AD, 66). The overarching rule is: *that there be possibilities is not itself one of the possibilities*. The character of concrete temporality is the creative advance into novelty, the cumulative actualization of possibility. But this lesser rule both requires and explains an exception. Thus: *that* there be the realization of novel alternatives is not one of the alternatives, and that there be the actualization of future possibilities is not itself one of the possibilities, but is an abstract *eternal* feature of time as creative advance. In this sense time requires eternity as its primordial and everlasting feature, and eternity requires time as the concrete whole of which it is an abstract generic feature.

4.2 *Modality is Essentially Temporal*

Having examined the thesis that time is objective modality, it is a relatively simple task to explain the converse thesis that modality is essentially temporal. Thus: the actual is the past, the possible is the future, and the necessary is the eternal.

4.2.1 Possibility is an Objective Mode of Temporal Process

To be possible means to be future. "Possibility and futurity are in principle one" (CS, 138). More succinctly, "the possible *is* the future" (CS, 61; my italics). Possibilities are *contingent* because they are competitive: the actualization of this possibility here and now excludes the actualization of that possibility here and now; red here-now excludes green here-now. Contingency means partial exclusivity or partial tolerance of possible states of affairs. Real futurity, and hence real possibility, has this character of contingency. "Possible," "future," and "contingent" are metaphysical synonyms for Hartshorne.[26]

By extending the notion of futurity to include all states of affairs that once were future, we may legitimately refer to past actualities as once-possible and therefore once-contingent. Granted the present state of world process, past actualities are *conditionally* necessary (cf. 4.3.3 below), but they remain contingent matters-of-fact in their origin. "Since the past contains a series of previous futures, it too involves possibility. Every 'today' was once 'tomorrow,' a limited range of open alternatives."[27]

4.2.2 Possibility and Actuality

The contrast between possibility and actuality highlights the indefinite, non-particular, non-individual character of potentialities. To be actual is, as we have seen, to be past, complete, definite, particular, individual, to be datum for further experience--in short, to be what Whitehead called "brute fact." But the "this" of an actuality has no advance status, because "there is no such thing as a possible particular....Possibilities are irreducibly non-particular" (CS, 61). Again, "creativity does not map the details of its future actions, even as possible" (CS, 65). In other words, the particularity and definiteness of individual events result from the free creative decision among possibilities, which constitutes the actualization of just *this* fact. The change from "merely possible" to "actual" "connotes 'some additional definiteness' not contained in any of the antecedently obtaining alternatives" (RSP, 98).

We have seen that to be past is to be a datum for some future experience: to be is to be a potential for every subsequent becoming. Now, "future experience" and "subsequent becoming" refer to the realm of possibility which is *in* actuality as effects are in their causes. This is to say that *the locus of possibility is in actuality*, just as the future is contained as outline in the present and the past. "The togetherness of actuality and possibility can only be in actuality. Indeed the possibility of the future is the same as the actuality of the past and present, in their character as destined to be included in some richer total reality. *The potentiality of an event is just the actuality of its predecessors*" (CS, 225; italics added).

In this sense, possibility refers to a real *capacity* of world process to produce a certain state of affairs. "Only what exists has the power to create further existence, and it has this power because what exists (a society) is not complete in all aspects but has an element of futurity, or a principle of self-transcendence, of being potentially what it as yet is not" (WP, 80). What *can* be is an aspect of what already *is*. To say that actuality is the locus of possibility is just to state once again the very nature of process as creative advance: namely, that actuality contains outlines or tendencies or horizons for further becoming.

It is an implication of this doctrine of the potential as an aspect of the existent that the distinction between logical possibility and real possibility must be stated very carefully. *In principle* there is no such distinction, although *in fact* some things may *seem* logically possible which are not really possible. Or, to put it another way, the distinction between logical possibility and real possibility is not a metaphysical distinction, but is a distinction which may arise from our limited (and so imperfect) understanding of world process. Let me explain.

A described state of affairs is *logically* possible if the description makes sense and involves no contradiction. For the state of affairs to be *really* possible, the minimal further requirement is that it qualify as one of the alternative future outcomes of the present stage of world process (or as one of the once-future outcomes of now-past states of affairs). In other words, a possibility cannot be *real* "unless it would, if actual, be an effect of a cause which is real, or the effect of a possible cause which if actual, would itself be the effect of a cause which...(the series ultimately terminating in a cause which is real)" (MVG, 304). The criterion for logical possibility, then, is non-contradiction; and the criterion for real possibility is compatibility with actuality.

But, in principle, are these criteria really different? To say that a concept is logically possible by virtue of its lack of self-contradiction is simply to say that the *meanings* involved in the concept do not contradict one another. But meanings have *references*, and so we must ask what are the references of these meanings which do not contradict one another?

> The meanings whose consistency is granted must mean something, and this referent of the meanings is not the consistency but the presupposition of there being any meanings, consistent or otherwise. If a consistent meaning means something, *but something not even possible*, then it means something very odd indeed. If it means only its own consistency, then it is really meaningless. (MVG, 304; italics added)

In other words, the non-contradictory *meanings* involved in genuinely logical possibilities must themselves refer at least to possibilities. What sort of possibilities? Obviously, at

some point, to *real* possibilities; for if the meanings involved
in logical possibility A refer to logical possibility B, and
the meanings involved in B refer to logical possibility C
and..., we have an infinite regress. *At some point the meanings involved in a logical possibility must refer at least to a
real possibility*. In short, compatibility with actuality
(either directly or indirectly, through compatibility with a
real capacity of actuality) is not only the definition of real
metaphysical potentiality, it is also the criterion for logical
conceivability, because a consistent thought cannot refer just
to its own consistency. "Logical and real are here correlative
and mutually explicative."[28]

We may conclude that the criterion of genuine conceivability (non-contradiction) and the criterion of real possibility
(compatibility with actuality) are, in principle, one and the
same. Strictly speaking, then, distinctions between real and
logical possibility are apparent only, and are a function of
imperfect knowledge: "it is only because of lack of clarity or
definiteness that really impossible descriptions appear to us
as logically possible. If we had perfect command of our ideas
we should see logical absurdity in any description that is
really impossible."[29] For example, "in the thought of one who
really grasped the full reality of the present situation S, the
causal limitations that S imposes on the future would, we may
surmise, be included in this grasp, and the notion of a violation of these limitations would be *contradictory*."[30]

(Note: Hartshorne does *not* argue that everything which is
logically possible will in fact be actualized, any more than he
argues that everything that is really possible will be actualized; possibilities--both real and logical--are wider than actuality, and the course of world process obviously excludes the
actualization of many possibilities. Rather, the argument is
that all real possibility has its logical correlate, and that
all genuine logical possibility has its real correlate: "*Any*
possibility is at some time real and future."[31] The implications of this doctrine for Hartshorne's theory of modality are
discussed in Chapter IV, section 2.)

4.2.3 Possibility and Necessity

If process is ultimate and temporal, then necessity cannot be "out of time." The temporal interpretation of possibility is therefore an indispensable prologue for understanding necessity. "If we really know what existential or ontological possibility is, then, and only then, we may be able to construe ontological necessity. It is easy to prove that the inclusive modality is possibility."[32] Just as the logician argues that necessary truth is truth in all possible worlds, so Hartshorne contends that ontological necessity is "the universal factor in possibility,"[33] "what will be in any possible case" (CS, 71), what is "common to all possibilities, hence neutral as to which possibility may be actualized" (AD, 80), "that which is common to a set of chances; or that of whose absence there is no chance" (RSP, 86). If the possible is the future, then "we can define the necessary as that which has *always* been part of the settled content of the future, and thus has never been and will never be an open possibility" (CS, 133). Again, "that which has always characterized the future in its aspect of will-be cannot be contingent."[34] (Note that on this temporal interpretation, "necessity" is not equivalent to "always so" if this is taken to mean, in every actual case, whether past or future. For, once again, there are no future actualities; the future is the realm of possibility. "Necessity," rather, means "impossibility of an alternative.")

If the necessary is a universal constituent of all possibility (and hence of all actuality), then the necessary is wholly *abstract*, totally lacking in the concrete richness of detail and variety. Necessity never refers to a particular state of affairs, but rather to a feature of all states of affairs. Necessary truths all have this character of abstract universality. For example, that "every effect has a cause" entails no particular state of affairs, but is entailed by every state of affairs. Likewise, the necessary existence of God will be highly abstract: "Necessary existence is not actuality plus something, some necessity or other. It is nothing actual at all, but an essence, embodied in any and every state of contingent actuality" (LP, 102). For just this reason

Hartshorne argues that the necessary divine existence cannot be the complete theistic truth, but must be a feature abstracted from contingent divine states or experiences (see below, Chapter III, section 4.1). "It is necessary that God be capable of contingent qualifications" (AD, 209).

In terms of the distinction between conditional and unconditional necessity (see above, section 1.2), Hartshorne summarizes his doctrine of time as objective modality in this way: "Eternity is the mode of absolute or abstract necessity and possibility, the past is the mode of conditional or concrete necessity (being necessary, given the actual present), the future is the mixed mode of conditional necessity and possibility" (CS, 253). Or, in other words, time contains, in addition to actuality and possibility, both conditional and unconditional necessities. Given the present state of the world, for example, we may regard its past history as conditionally necessary. Past actualities will always have been just what they have been. Napoleon's defeat at Waterloo is conditionally necessary in this sense. Also, given the present state of affairs, we may regard some features of the immediate future as conditionally necessary or impossible: I cannot take a train that is not scheduled to run tomorrow.

But temporal process also contains unconditional or absolute necessities, and these are the *eternal* features of temporality. For example, *that there be temporal process* is an unconditional or eternal truth about reality. The only alternatives to process are either nothing at all or pure being without becoming, both of which are nonsensical states of affairs (see above, 1.3 and 2.2). There is, for Hartshorne, no conceivable alternative to process, and so process itself depends upon no conditions; it is unconditionally necessary.

Because process is unconditionally necessary, it follows that what is required by process (or true of process as such) is *also* unconditionally necessary. Or, in other words, because process depends upon no conditions, it cannot itself be considered a condition, as if we could say that metaphysical truths are necessary, *assuming* process. This is exactly what is denied by the notion of unconditional necessity. "Further

process adds only new specializations; what is already pervasive of the possibilities can never cease to be so."[35] It is
this sense of absolute necessity which is at issue in the ontological argument. The divine existence is, Hartshorne argues,
an unconditionally necessary and eternal feature of process
(see below, Chapter V, objection 2a).

This Hartshornean analysis of possibility as an objective
mode of temporality, as a metaphysical feature of actuality,
and as the inclusive whole in terms of which necessity is to be
understood profoundly affects his treatment of the ontological
argument. I turn now to the employment of that theory in
Hartshorne's reconception of divinity (Chapter III) and in his
modal theory (Chapter IV).

CHAPTER II

[1]Charles Hartshorne, "Santayana's Doctrine of Essence," *The Philosophy of George Santayana*, ed. Paul A. Schilpp (New York: Tudor Publishing, 1940), p. 149.

[2]A. N. Whitehead, *Process and Reality* (New York: Free Press, 1969), p. 7.

[3]Antony Flew, "Theology and Falsification," in *New Essays in Philosophical Theology*, ed. Antony Flew and Alasdair MacIntyre (New York: Macmillan, 1955), pp. 96-99.

[4]Ibid., p. 98. See also Antony Flew, *God and Philosophy* (New York: Dell Publishing, 1966), pp. 21-22.

[5]See, for example, Hartshorne's article, "Real Possibility," *The Journal of Philosophy* 60/21 (October 10, 1963), 594-95; also, *Creative Synthesis and Philosophic Method* (LaSalle, IL: Open Court, 1970), p. 68, and *Anselm's Discovery*, p. 168.

[6]See also the discussion of necessary existential statements in Chapter IV, section 1.

[7]See below, section 2.1 ("Necessarily, Experience Occurs") and section 2.2 ("Necessarily, Creative Synthesis Occurs").

[8]A. N. Whitehead, *Adventures of Ideas* (New York: Free Press, 1967), p. 158.

[9]Hartshorne offers the following as synonyms for "actual entity": "least unit of process," "unit-becoming," "unit-happening," "unit-event," and "quantum-process" (WP, 119-20).

[10]See below, Chapter IV, section 3.5.2.

[11]Whitehead, *Process and Reality*, p. 184.

[12]Ibid., p. 193.

[13]Hartshorne is continually warning against confusion on this point. He writes, for example: "'Inherent in experience as such' means exactly what it says; 'inherent in *human* experience as such' would mean something else, and those who can see no great difference are probably not fitted for metaphysical inquiry" (CS, 25).

[14]The change from experienc*ing* to experienc*ed* is not in the actuality, since being experienced is an external relation for the actuality, although an internal relation for the new subject.

[15]"And again, please note that '*human* experience' is restrictive, rather than a harmless redundancy" (CS, 26).

[16]Whitehead, *Process and Reality*, p. 26.

[17]A world totally lacking in order is, for Hartshorne, nonsense. He writes: "Of course, we can take the impossibility of this as a mere tautology, in that the word 'world' connotes an existing order. But it remains to ask what, if anything, we can really think corresponding to the sentence, 'No world, no real order, exists.' Is this not an absolutely unconfirmable proposition? The possibility of confirmation implies an order of some sort" (LP, 283).

[18]Hartshorne, "Santayana's Doctrine of Essence," p. 146.

[19]See below, Chapter III, section 4.2.

[20]Morris R. Cohen, *A Preface to Logic* (New York: Meridian Books, 1956), pp. 87-89. Cohen writes: "Philosophically it [the principle of polarity] may be generalized as the principle, not of the identity, but of the necessary copresence and mutual dependence of opposite determinations. It warns us against the greatest bane of philosophizing, to wit: the easy artificial dilemma between unity and plurality, rest and motion, substance and function, actual and ideal, etc." (p. 88).

[21]This definition is not to be taken as materially different from the definition examined above in 1.1. What is true of concreteness as such is obviously an unconditionally necessary existential truth. As Hartshorne writes: "Diverse as these formulae may seem at first glance, I believe that they all imply the same thing and differ only in emphasis and focus of explicitness" (CS, 24).

[22]*Confessions*, Book XI, esp. sections 14-31.

[23]See n. 9.

[24]As Whitehead cryptically remarked: "The vast causal independence of contemporary occasions is the preservative of the elbow-room in the universe" (*Adventures of Ideas*, p. 195). Or again, "the causal independence of contemporary occasions is the ground for the freedom within the Universe" (ibid., p. 198).

[25]In other words, since contemporary entities do not prehend one another, all prehension is of the immediate past, and so is a short-range version of memory, i.e., experience of *past* experience.

[26]Strictly speaking, we must distinguish two senses of "possible" if the statement is to be entirely correct; for it is true that God is in a sense possible (i.e., not impossible), although he is not contingent. Hartshorne's distinction between "pure" or "eternal" possibilities and "spatio-temporally localized" possibilities is to the point here: "If something is

eternally possible, then this is a necessary not a contingent truth. No choice, decision, or selection is presupposed. But what is possible here and now depends upon what has previously happened, including the arbitrary decisions previously made" (AD, 185). In short, the possibility of God is not a possibility of the second kind, because with eternal things to be possible and to be are the same (see above, pp. 4-5).

[27] Charles Hartshorne, "Necessity," *The Review of Metaphysics* 21/2 (December 1967), 293.

[28] Hartshorne, "Real Possibility," p. 598.

[29] Ibid., p. 594.

[30] Ibid., p. 603; italics added.

[31] Ibid., p. 597; italics added.

[32] Hartshorne, "Necessity," p. 292.

[33] Ibid., p. 294.

[34] Ibid.

[35] Ibid.

CHAPTER III

POSSIBILITY AND DIVINITY

"Anselm's main mistake is in his idea of God itself, not in his proof" (AD, 106). Anselm's principle, as we have seen, is the insight that God or "perfect being" could exist only necessarily if it exists at all. "If it can be conceived at all, it must exist" (*Reply*, I). Unfortunately, says Hartshorne, Anselm spoiled his discovery by misconceiving the idea of perfect being. Anselm, and the classical tradition in general, interpreted perfection as *actus purus*. Therefore we can salvage the Anselmian discovery only by reconceiving the idea of divinity. "Anselm's reasoning, when its logic is sufficiently carefully attended to, illuminates not only the existence but the nature of God. It requires us to reconceive the import of 'divine'" (AD, 9-10).

In this chapter I turn to an examination of Hartshorne's reconception of God in an effort to justify the central assumption in his ontological proof, namely, that the existence of God is possible. This assumption is central, because, to state the interior logic of the argument once again, in the case of absolutely necessary existence, to be possible and to be are the same (see above, Chapter I, section 2.1). The thesis to be defended here is twofold: (a) that the key to Hartshorne's theistic doctrine is the inclusion of possibility in the reality of God, and (b) that this neoclassical conception of God is able to overcome the major logical and metaphysical difficulties which afflict the traditional philosophical understanding of God. After (1) a brief description of what Hartshorne means by the classical and the neoclassical understandings of God, I will (2) turn to an inspection of a formal ambiguity in the notion of perfection. I will then compare critically the traditional and the Hartshornean interpretations of perfection, paying particular attention (3) to Hartshorne's metaphysical argument that perfection requires potentiality and (4) to his logical argument that the abstract quality of perfection requires concrete perfect states. I will conclude (5) by noting the import of these investigations for the ontological proof.

1. Classical and Neoclassical Understandings
of Divinity

The ontological argument, being a metaphysical argument, employs a philosophical understanding of the reality of God. What is a philosopher to mean when he uses the word "God"? Is there any philosophically neutral translation of the religious significance of this name? Hartshorne suggests that the philosophical term "perfect" or "perfect being" is faithful to the deepest religious import of the scriptural witness, for only a perfect being will be completely worthy of religious worship (NT, 1ff.).

So the question is, what do we mean, philosophically speaking, by a perfect being? There have been, and are, many different answers to this question in the history of Eastern and Western thought. In his book, *Philosophers Speak of God*, Hartshorne develops what I will call *typologies* or *motifs* which distinguish various schools of interpretation of the meaning of perfection. These typologies are more systematic than historical, which is to say that Hartshorne analyzes and criticizes historical texts for the explicit purpose of sketching the broad outlines of different *types* of interpretations of perfection. Some examples of these typologies are: Aristotelian theism, classical theism, classical pantheism, logico-metaphysical skepticism, psychological skepticism, and (Hartshorne's own approach) neoclassical theism or panentheism.

The two typologies that we will concentrate on in this chapter are those that Hartshorne calls classical theism and neoclassical theism. There are two reasons for this exclusive concern. In the first place, classical theism represents an understanding of divinity that has largely dominated Western theology, and most of Hartshorne's arguments supporting the need for a new, neoclassical, understanding are made vis-à-vis this traditional approach to the question of perfection. In the second place, and more directly to the point of this inquiry, Hartshorne understands Anselm to be a classical theist. And Hartshorne's argument against Anselm is that, while his insight into the logical *status* of perfection was correct (i.e., that perfection is either absolutely necessary or utterly impossible), his interpretation of what perfection *means* was inadequate. Neoclassicism is offered as a more adequate interpretation. This is an important shift in an argument whose central premise is the conceivability of perfection.

Classical theism, which Hartshorne at other times calls "traditional theism," is a typology which includes such diverse thinkers as Philo, Augustine, Anselm, Aquinas and Leibniz (PSG, 17). Historically speaking, Hartshorne argues, what draws these various thinkers together is their common attempt to interpret the scriptural understanding of God in terms of Greek (chiefly Aristotelian) metaphysics. What we find in all these thinkers is a "double insistence upon divine absoluteness and omniscient providence" (PSG, 76), the former reflecting the Greek idea of the self-sufficiency and independence (*aseitas*) of deity, the latter mirroring "the scriptural tenets of creation and providential concern with respect to the world" (PSG, 76).

Systematically speaking, the theme which is common to these men is the basic assumption that *perfection must imply changelessness*. Change must be for better or for worse, and in either case a being who changes could not be perfect, for perfection cannot become "more" perfect (else it was not originally perfect), nor, obviously, can it become "less" perfect (for then it is no longer perfect). The strictly metaphysical way of putting this point is to say that a perfect being cannot have any merely potential aspects, for potentiality is precisely the capacity to change. Or, to put it the other way, a perfect being must be *wholly actual*.

For Hartshorne's purposes, then, what unites, for example, Augustine, Anselm and Aquinas into an identifiable "school" of thought is their denial of all metaphysical potentiality in the reality of God. Whatever other differences there may be among them, they all agree to the proposition that, as Thomas expressed it, "the first being must of necessity be in act, and in no way in potentiality" (S.T., I, 3, a.1). This is what Hartshorne calls the *actus purus* interpretation of divine perfection, "that is, a reality in which nothing positive is left merely potential" (CS, 229).

Many of the divine attributes, as classically interpreted, follow from this motif of the denial of potentiality in God. For example, as we have already pointed out, God is *immutable*. He is also *eternal* in the sense that he exists outside the order of possibilities, that is, outside of time. He is without accidents (these being qualifications of an individual that are subject to change), and so is wholly *necessary*. There is thus no distinction between *what* he is and *that* he is; he is simple, uncomposed, without parts, or, as Thomas put it, his essence is his existence.

No doubt much could be, and has been, written concerning the complexities and subtleties of the classical understanding of God. But in terms of an identifiable systematic approach to the question of what perfection means, I take Hartshorne's point here to be essentially correct: the metaphysical lynchpin in this classical conception of deity is the exclusion of potentiality from the Godhead.

Neoclassical theism is offered by Hartshorne as a clear-cut alternative to the classical interpretation of perfection. The neoclassical motif is sponsored chiefly by Whitehead and Hartshorne, although historical roots are claimed in Schelling, Fechner, Peirce and Berdyaev. The constructive or systematic link among these thinkers is the argument that perfection need *not* imply complete changelessness. Intuitively speaking, the point is this: all our experience contradicts the assumption that perfection means sheer actual completeness involving no change, and therefore no real relations to others. On the contrary, Hartshorne suggests, the better a man is, the *greater* his ability to adapt to new situations, to be related to new concerns, to include new interests—all the while preserving his integral identity. The "perfect" man is the man who can assume, without loss of individual identity, many various roles (roles which require real internal relations, and hence real capacity for change and adaptation)—e.g., father, husband, attorney, etc. It would seem then that "the higher integrity must go with the greater variety or complexity," so that perfection itself would be "the uttermost permanence with the supreme capacity for change" (RSP, 137). Therefore, "perfection

does not mean a zero, but a maximum, of potentiality, of unactualized power to be" (LP, 37).

Thus, *the key move in the Hartshornean reconception of God
is precisely the introduction of possibility into the Godhead.*
Actus purus is reinterpreted on the model of *modal coextensiveness*: God covers, with complete adequacy and comprehensiveness
(i.e., "perfectly") the territory of the actual *and* the territory of the possible. For example, God knows all actuality as
actual and all possibility as possible. "Perfection is modal
completeness, not actual completeness" (AD, 123).

Certain conclusions as to the nature and attributes of God
follow directly from this inclusion of potentiality in the
reality of God. For example, God cannot be wholly simple, because the distinction between his actuality and his possibility,
between what he *is* and what he *can be*, is a real distinction in
God's nature. Modal coextensiveness "implies a distinction...
between an individual (a) in its abstract identity and (b) in
its concrete actual states" (LP, 65). Hartshorne thus expands
the traditional duality of essence (*what* an individual is) and
existence (*that* an individual is) into a triad: essence, existence, and *actuality* (*how*, or in what state, the individual
exists). While agreeing with the classical doctrine that God's
essence is his existence, Hartshorne maintains *in addition* that
the divine essence-existence is distinct from the divine actuality (we may thus speak simply of the existence-actuality distinction, since this is the point of difference in the two doctrines). "One must admit a real distinction (real for God, not
just for us) between abstract individuality or existence (these
are the same) and full concrete actuality (which is quite different)" (NT, 37).

The existence-actuality distinction provides a new analogy
for understanding the divine nature. In every individual,
divine and non-divine, we may distinguish between existence and
actuality (see Chapter II, section 2.1). This is the distinction, for example, between the truth *that* I exist, and the fact
that I exist *now* in the concrete state of writing this chapter,
rather than playing or sleeping. Or again, it is the distinction between the abstract characteristics of my identity (that

I am a man, that I was born of such-and-such parents, that I am a theologian, etc.) and the concrete states in which those features are expressed. "Existence" thus means *somehow actualized*, and requires only the non-emptiness of the appropriate class of concrete actualities. "'Existence' is merely a relation of exemplification which actuality (any suitable actuality) has to essence" (AD, 131).

What makes the analogy an *analogy* and preserves the "infinite qualitative difference" between God and man is simply this: in all cases *except* the divine, existence as well as actuality is contingent.[1] For example, it is a contingent truth not only that I should be writing this paper now, but that I should even *be* at all. In the divine case, however, while the actual states are contingent, the *existence* is unconditionally necessary: *that* the class of divine states cannot be empty is a strictly necessary truth. "Neoclassical theism... distinguishes existence and actuality, and does this in reference not only to God but to all things. What is exceptional about God is that in Him alone is it possible to treat existence as not only different, but different *modally*, from actuality, i.e., so that the one is necessary, the other contingent" (AD, 78).

It follows, on Hartshorne's interpretation, therefore, that all the properties classically attributed to God--necessity, immutability, eternity, infinity--apply to only one aspect of the divine nature, namely to his essence-existence, and not to his contingent, developing, temporal, finite actual states. The classical theistic properties are not denied; rather, they are taken as abstractions from the concrete reality of God, and hence as half-truths, not final or complete truths, about the divine nature.

In sum, Hartshorne's neoclassical interpretation of perfection has two central features: the doctrine of modal coextensiveness and the distinction between the divine existence and the divine actuality.

Of course, the mere juxtaposition of the two doctrines of God does not adjudicate their relative adequacy. I intend to address this point in the remainder of the chapter. For the

present, my aim has been simply to establish the thesis that
the exclusion versus the inclusion of potentiality in the di-
vine nature is the major metaphysical issue involved in the
traditional and the Hartshornean conceptions of God. *Actus*
purus is a doctrine which excludes all potentiality--and hence
all temporality, change and contingency--from the reality of
God; modal coextensiveness is a doctrine which argues that perfection must be conceived as inclusive of all possibility as
well as of all actuality.

I turn now to the second thesis: that *the Hartshornean*
conception of God is able to resolve the major logical and
metaphysical problems attending the classical doctrine of actus
purus. The case for this thesis will be developed in three
steps: first, from purely formal considerations on the logic of
the notion of perfection; second, from the metaphysical argument that perfection requires potentiality (this corresponds to
Hartshorne's doctrine of modal coextensiveness); third, from
the logical argument that the abstract concept of perfection
requires concrete perfect states (this corresponds to Hartshorne's distinction between the divine existence and the divine
actuality).

2. A Formal Ambiguity in the Notion of Perfection

The issue before us concerns the relative merits of including or excluding metaphysical potentiality in the reality
of God. The first point to be established is simple but
crucial: we cannot argue, "God is perfect, and *therefore* must
exist without possibility of change." For, as Hartshorne has
pointed out, the notion of perfection is subtly ambiguous.

2.1 *The Ambiguity of "Perfection"*

Anselm spoke of God as "that than which none greater can
be conceived." The definition thus has to do with unsurpassability, so that the minimal requirement for God's perfection
is that "he has no possible rival (no equal or superior) among
individuals. He could not be equaled or excelled by another"
(PSG, 9). The point seems obvious, but it is hardly trivial;

for there is a neoclassical as well as a classical way of interpreting unsurpassability. It may mean (a) that God is unsurpassable by any, or (b) that God is unsurpassable by any, *save self in future states*. Put another way, the "none" in "none greater can be conceived" may mean: (a) no entity other than the being (said to be perfect) as it actually is, or it may mean (b) no being other than the being (said to be perfect) as it either is *or else could be or become*. The distinction is important: "According to the first meaning (which follows automatically if one assumes that the perfect can have no potential states--an assumption not deducible from the mere idea of 'none greater,' because of the latter's equivocal connotation) the perfect is *unsurpassable in conception or possibility even by itself*; according to the second meaning it is *unsurpassable except by itself*" (MVG, 7). Hartshorne suggests the technical terms "absolute perfection" (A perfection) for the first or absolute unsurpassability, and "relative perfection" (R perfection) for the second or self-surpassing unsurpassability (MVG, 7). "Perfect" and "perfectible" or "statically perfect" and "dynamically perfect" express the same distinction.

Three points are worthy of note: first, the ambiguity is a purely logical feature of "perfection" or "unsurpassability" or "none," and therefore, second, the issue of God's inclusion of potential states cannot be resolved negatively merely by invoking the requirements of perfection or unsurpassability--for the ambiguity of the requirements themselves is precisely the point at issue. Third, there is no *prima facie* evidence that the second interpretation of perfection as "the self-surpassing surpasser of all" fails to meet the religious demand for perfection. Why, asks Hartshorne, should it offend the religious sensibility if God can surpass himself in future states, provided he cannot be surpassed or even rivaled by any *other* being?

2.2 *The Neglected Alternative*

It follows from this ambiguity in the notion of perfection that the disjunction, either God is absolutely perfect or he is not perfect (and hence there is no God), is really too simple.

The thinker in mere dichotomies is, as Peirce said, a crude fellow, trying to make delicate dissections with an ax. "God is absolutely perfect in all respects" and "God is absolutely perfect in no respects" are logical contraries; therefore, while only one can be true, both can be false. The "neglected alternative" here is what lies between "all" and "none," namely, "some." Hence the second (purely formal) point of our inquiry into the conception of God: *all* the formally possible doctrines must be considered. "Almost everything depends upon the adequacy of the philosopher's survey of the possibilities ...if all the formal possibilities are not controlled, we not only run the risk of fallaciously inferring the truth of one view from the difficulties of some only of its possible rivals, but we also run the risk of trying to answer a perhaps meaningless question, namely, which of two falsehoods (or absurdities) is more false?" (MVG, 33).

Now the formal possibilities in the case we are considering are three and not two: (1) God is *in all respects* absolutely perfect or unsurpassable, and in no way perfectible or surpassable by self; (2) God is *in some respects* absolutely perfect and unsurpassable, and *in other respects* perfectible or surpassable by self; (3) God is in no respects absolutely perfect, and in all respects perfectible. Or symbolically, A, AR, R. (I will assume without extended argument that type-three theism cannot serve as a valid option; for a "God" in no respect absolutely perfect and in all respects perfectible would not differ essentially from man, whose striving for perfection consists in the ethical attempt to surpass himself in future states.) "There is no more rigorous trichotomy than that of 'all, some, none'; hence the question, *Is God absolutely perfect in all, in some, or in no respects*? is as rigorous a division of the theological problem as can be given if any use at all is to be made of the idea of perfection" (MVG, 33). The value of this position matrix, then, is not that it resolves the issue of whether or not potentiality is to be included in the divine reality, but that it guarantees that an affirmative answer is not simply overlooked.

3. Perfection Requires Potentiality:
the Metaphysical Arguments

I have noted two central features in Hartshorne's concept of God: the doctrine of modal coextensiveness and the existence-actuality distinction. In this section we will consider the idea of modal coextensiveness, a doctrine which is derived from the metaphysical argument that "the idea of perfection, when coherently defined...requires that there be potentiality as well as actuality."[2]

Hartshorne's interpretation of perfection as modal coextensiveness (rather than as *actus purus*) is simply a specification, in terms of *divine* reality, of his general metaphysical argument that *all* reality has the character of creative synthesis or process. Whereas *actus purus* expresses the divine perfection in terms of a metaphysics of being, modal coextensiveness expresses that perfection in terms of a metaphysics of becoming. Thus the arguments for modal coextensiveness depend upon exactly the same principles as the arguments supporting a metaphysics of process, such as that becoming can include being, but not *vice versa* (see Chapter II, section 2.2). If the ultimate metaphysical principle is not being, but becoming-as-*including*-being, then reality has two aspects, and a perfect being will be the perfection of both aspects, concrete becoming and abstract being: this is Hartshorne's argument. In one respect (the abstract) the perfect being will be maximally or statically perfect, but in another respect (the concrete) the perfect being will be dynamically perfect or maximally perfectible, and thus completely coextensive with metaphysical potentiality. In short, perfection will be, in one respect, supremely changeless, and, in another, supremely changing; for *perfection as sheer changelessness can be only the abstract dimension of perfection as infinite capacity to change*. Abstract changelessness implies a concrete changing whole in the same way that being implies becoming.

That perfection must be modal completeness is, therefore, a doctrine having the same logical status as the doctrine that reality is social process. As Hartshorne expresses it in one place, the question of divine perfection "is the social question taken at its maximum" (RSP, 184). This motif lies at the basis of the following specific arguments.

3.1 *Actuality and Possibility*

The *actus purus* doctrine entails a collapse in the distinction between possibility and actuality. The doctrine that God possesses all possible value *as actual* "makes possibility and actuality completely coextensive and for all purposes identical" (RSP, 117). Thus to accept the *actus purus* interpretation of perfection is also to accept the view that our radical experience of possibility--that is, of change, contingency and futurity--is a mere anthropomorphism. For if from the point of view of the ultimate knower there is no distinction between actual and possible, then some of our most fundamental experiences are really illusions. But if process or becoming (i.e., the cumulative actualization of possibility) is the ultimate character of reality (as we argued in Chapter II), then actuality and possibility cannot be identical, but must remain irreducibly and modally distinct. Therefore, we must choose between *actus purus* and creative becoming; we cannot have it both ways, for their logics are incompatible.

Consider, by way of illustration, the traditional interpretation of omniscience: God, from the viewpoint of eternity, knows the future (which to us is hidden) much as a pilot surveys from above the whole stretch of a mountain range which is only gradually revealed to the pedestrian below. The assumption here is that the future contains antecedently real events or definite actualities, which are capable of being known as definite and as actual by a perfect knower. In short, the distinction between actual and possible vanishes from the divine viewpoint.

Not only is this surrender of future possibility a high price to pay for an interpretation of omniscience, it is a wholly unreasonable price; for the traditional interpretation simply begs the question concerning the ultimate ontological status of possibility by assuming that perfection--and hence perfect knowledge--excludes all potentiality. "The Thomistic doctrine that divine knowledge of our future acts is not of acts future to God's knowing, but, as it were, simultaneous with his eternity (since his knowing is not 'before' or 'after' but above time altogether) simply assumes that time has a settled character from the standpoint of eternity--which is the basic question at issue" (RSP, 201).

But consider: if omniscience is correctly described as "perfect knowledge" or as "knowledge completely adequate to reality"; and if the indeterminacy which is of the essence of events, until they are present or past, is objectively involved in temporality itself, then a perfect knower will know the future as partially indeterminate, as possible and not as actual. God's knowledge is perfect because he knows all actuality as actual and all possibility as possible. "God as omniscient must actually know as actual all that is actual; he must also be *capable* of knowing as actual anything that could be actual."[3]

In short, the doctrine of modal coextensiveness is able to avoid the wholly unwarranted collapse of the distinction between actual and possible. Thus, for example, our conception of God need not require us to view our experience of future possibility as an anthropomorphic handicap. We need not deny this experience; we need only insist that whereas we know *some* actuality more or less clearly and *some* possibility more or less vaguely, God knows *all* actuality perfectly and *all* possibility with as great an amount of clarity as the present stage of world process admits. "Thus we may define perfection as modal *coincidence*, and we may interpret this under the analogy of infallible knowledge" (LP, 38).[4]

3.2 *Incompossibles*

In the second place, as Leibniz argued, the simultaneous actualization of all possible value is itself a metaphysical impossibility. Options which are possible disjunctively are not all possible conjunctively; there are incompossible possibilities. Red here-now excludes green here-now. By what principle of rational or intelligible discourse, then, can we simply suspend Leibniz's law of incompossibles in the divine case?

The answer is: we need not suspend the law. On the modal coextensiveness model, to say that God is perfect will not mean

that he actualizes all possible value, but that he includes all
actual value as actual, and all possible value as possible.
"He is infinitely capable of actuality, rather than infinitely
actual" (NT, 21). In this way we avoid the problem of incompossibles: "God's uniqueness is not that He exhaustively actualizes all possible value (this is impossible), but that there
is no consistent set of possible values He could not enjoy"
(AD, 218).

3.3 *Actuality and Infinity*

Both classical and neoclassical theists hold that God is
in some sense infinite. But only the neoclassical typology, it
seems, can provide a consistent metaphysical explanation of *how*
God is infinite. We must ask how, on the classical interpretation, *actus purus* could entail infinity. If the metaphysical
meaning of actuality is "decision among competitive alternative
possibilities," then it is certain that the range of unactualized possibilities is always larger than the range of chosen
actualities. If actuality could be infinite, what are we to
say about the range of unactualized possibilities? Is it
"larger" than infinity?

Or does the "actuality" in *actus purus* mean something
other than "actualization of exclusive possibilities," and, if
so, what? The only available alternative meaning, it seems, is
"the actualization of *all* possibilities"--but now we are back
to Leibniz's problem of incompossibles. An absolute maximum of
actuality in this sense is as problematic as the notion of a
greatest possible number.

It seems, then, that what is metaphysically infinite is
not the totality of actuality, but the unrestricted disjunction
of all possible states of affairs.[5] "Actuality and finitude
belong together, possibility and infinity belong together" (NT,
21). Thus we guarantee, rather than prevent, the literal infinity of God precisely by conceiving him as completely coextensive, not only with the totality of actuality (any amount
of which is finite), but also with the absolutely infinite
realm of possibility. "The 'unlimitedness' of God is in his
contingent potential aspects, not his actuality" (CS, 158).

3.4 *Actuality and Necessity*

Nor can the divine reality--conceived as wholly actual--be necessary. No actuality, even a "pure" actuality, can be necessary, and this is the insight which has been misstated in the dogma that "existence is not a predicate." *Modality* of existence is indeed always a predicate, for every existent exists either necessarily or contingently. What is *not* a predicate and is in no case necessary is the particular, concrete, momentary, contingent state which embodies the abstract existence. Actuality, being the realization of *this* possibility rather than *that*, is always--even in the divine case--a logical surd. "No actuality, no particular *how* of concretization, can be necessary" (AD, 217). Conclusion: God *as actual* cannot be necessary.

But note: the class of divine states can be *necessarily* non-empty, even though all its actual or potential members are contingent. On the neoclassical interpretation the necessity of God is not in his actuality, but in his existence which ranges over all actual and possible states of affairs, so that the only alternative to an actuality embodying deity is another actuality also embodying deity. "If *all* possibility is a thing's own potential possession, then, whatever possibility is actualized, the thing must exist to possess this actualization. (Complete) modal coincidence entails necessary existence" (LP, 77).

To explore this insight further, however, we need to turn to Hartshorne's arguments regarding the concrete and abstract dimensions of deity.

4. The Existence-Actuality Distinction

Thus far I have argued in support of the first major feature of Hartshorne's doctrine of God, namely, that perfection is best conceived, not as *actus purus*, but as modal coextensiveness with actuality and possibility. This conclusion is warranted not only by a formal ambiguity in the notion of perfection, but also by material metaphysical considerations: the ultimate distinction between actuality and possibility, the

Leibnizian law of incompossibles, the infinity and the necessity of God--all require the divine perfection to be conceived as coextensive with *possibility* itself, as well as with actuality.

I turn now to the second feature of Hartshorne's reconception of divinity: the existence-actuality distinction, a distinction, Hartshorne says, which "is so essential that I would have little interest in the ontological proof apart from it."[6] That the doctrine of modal coextensiveness entails this distinction can be seen in the following way: if there is potentiality as well as actuality in the divine reality, then we *must* affirm the legitimacy of divine states, for (and this is the whole point of the metaphysical critique of *actus purus*) *God's actual state is not the greatest possible state*. "The accidents of God come under the genus of possible states of God" (MVG, 133). The same conclusion may be reached by another route, namely, that perfection has absolute and relative aspects. God is absolutely perfect in his abstract identity or existence, and so is absolutely unrivaled by any other individual; whereas God in his concrete actual states is relatively perfect or perfectible, and so is surpassable only by future states of himself. Thus the existence-actuality distinction follows from the idea of modal coextensiveness.

4.1 *Abstract and Concrete*

But there is yet another, and purely logical, consideration which urges the existence-actuality distinction, and it is this consideration and its implications and ramifications that I want to explore in this section of the chapter. This consideration is the logical distinction between concrete and abstract. The *actus purus* and modal coextensiveness interpretations share one feature in common, which is that they are both wholly *abstract* conceptions of perfection, definable *a priori* without reference to empirical realities. On the *actus purus* interpretation *whatever* value is so much as even possible God possesses as actual; on the modal coextensiveness interpretation *whatever* value is actual God possesses as actual, and *whatever* value is possible God possesses as possible. But these *a priori*

definitions raise a serious logical problem, which only the
neoclassical idea can avoid.

The problem is this: how a property definable *a priori*,
perfection, can be distinguished from and yet logically entail
an existent being *having* the property. This is one of the
strongest intuitive objections to the ontological argument:
what is the "bridge" from the *abstract* concept of perfection
to the *concrete* actuality of a perfect being? "Humanity," for
example, does not entail the existence of any particular man
embodying the concept, and why should it be different in the
case of perfection? Or again, humanity is not human, so why
should perfection be perfect?

The answer, on the neoclassical view, is as follows: (1)
The distinction between the divine existence and the divine actuality is a distinction between what *is* perfect and what *has*
the property of perfection. God *is* indeed his perfection, but
only in his abstract existence, i.e., his self-identical individuality. But God-*now*, God in his concrete states, *embodies*
perfection, "and is therefore not identical with it, being one
of its exemplifications" (LP, 105). "What 'has' the divine
perfection is not the divine individuality, in its fixed,
eternally identical character; for that is not an instance,
but is the divine perfection itself. It is the de facto states
which 'have' or instance perfection, rather than 'being' it"
(LP, 66). (2) Now, what *has* the property of perfection, the de
facto state, is, by definition, "perfect," and therefore cannot
be surpassed by any state of any *other* individual, but only by
future (perfect) states of the *same* individual. God-now and
God-tomorrow can be states only of the same individual. "Perfection is not a class of similar individuals, but only a class
of similar and genetically related states of one individual"
(LP, 67). (3) Therefore, in the unique case of perfection,
"the line between property and instance falls only between
individual and state, not also, as it usually does, between
individual and some broader class property, such as humanity"
(LP, 67). The bridge from abstract to concrete here is the
insight that the abstract property of perfection and the concrete instances of perfection must be features of the selfsame

individual. What the ontological argument proves is not the
fallacious conclusion that there is a necessary *instance* of
perfection, but rather (a) that the class of instances necessarily cannot be void and (b) that the entire class of instances must belong to one individual only.

This analysis rests on the neoclassical insistence that
we admit a distinction between the abstract divine existence
and concrete divine states. Classical thought, which does not
admit the distinction (for actual states imply further *potential* states) must face the consequences. The chief consequence
is that the ontological proof misfires when we employ the *actus
purus* doctrine. And "misfires" means more than "fails to prove
necessary existence," it means "establishes necessary *non-*
existence"--which is no small consequence.[7] The proof misfires
for a very obvious logical reason: a definition of perfection
that excludes divine states *guarantees* that there will be
nothing actual to embody the abstract concept.

The failure to draw the distinction between God's abstract
existence and his concrete actuality leaves the *actus purus*
doctrine open to three related problems: (1) *Actus purus* commits the homological fallacy of making a predicate an instance
of itself. (2) The classical God is, logically speaking,
wholly abstract: "if God does not have, but is His perfection,
then He is evidently the mere content of an abstract definition" (LP, 105). *Actus purus* thus falls prey to the paradox of
the abstractness of the necessary (J. N. Findlay) by assuming
that what is wholly necessary, and therefore wholly abstract,
can yet be actual. "One rule which is as surely logical as
any, the rule that the necessary must be abstract, empty, entailed by all the concrete or actual details of existence, but
entailing none, is set aside in classical theism by a mere
fiat. God *must* be actual, not a mere abstraction, and yet also
wholly necessary. For *this* exception no rule is possible" (AD,
67-68). Therefore (3), *actus purus* commits "the fallacy of
misplaced concreteness" (Whitehead) by confusing abstract properties with concrete realities.

What all these criticisms have in common is the charge
that classical theism ignores the distinction between property

and instance, or between individual identity and actual state, or--generally speaking--between *abstract* dimensions and *concrete* realities. Only the neoclassical idea can preserve these indispensable distinctions by employing the essence-existence-actuality analogy of the self. Thus the homological fallacy is avoided: perfection is perfect only in the sense that all concrete instances of perfection are instances of the same individual, whose abstract identity *is*, therefore, the abstract property of perfection. The distinction also dissolves Findlay's paradox: God is (in his essence-existence) wholly necessary, but he is not for all that a mere abstraction, for his necessity is an abstraction *from* inclusive, concrete divine states. The same distinction avoids the fallacy of misplaced concreteness: God "refers to a being conceived as having two aspects: an abstract eternal nature which is strictly necessary, and a total concrete, *de facto* actuality, containing both the eternal nature and successive accidental qualities" (LP, 149).

Two further Hartshornean objections to the classical doctrine of God derive from its failure to distinguish abstract and concrete in deity.

4.2 *Monopolarity*

One of the peculiar characteristics of the *actus purus* doctrine is the favoritism it manifests for one side only of each categorial contrast. Thus, for example, God is conceived as wholly necessary, meaning in no respect contingent, as wholly eternal and in no sense temporal, as wholly absolute and in no sense relative, etc. Hartshorne has called this a "monopolar" conception of deity, referring to the exception taken to the law of polarity that ultimate contraries are mutually interdependent, and so meaningless in isolation.

What is peculiar here is the lack of any logical or experiential evidence which warrants the monopolar interpretation. Classical theologians apparently understood the contrast, superior-inferior, simply to *coincide* with other categorial contrasts, so that, for example, being is superior and becoming inferior. The obvious conclusion from this line of reasoning is that the *most* superior being must manifest one pole only of each categorial contrast, namely the so-called "superior" pole. But why pursue this line of reasoning at all? Consider:

In the first place, if necessity, for example, is simply superior to contingency, then God will be *wholly* necessary and so wholly non-contingent. But what does "necessity" mean here? If "necessity" *ordinarily* means "an abstract feature of a concrete contingent whole," then necessity without *any* reference to contingency means something quite different. The two uses of "necessity" are completely equivocal, and we have surrendered the right to speak even analogically. "It is at best problematic whether the 'superior' pole retains its *meaning* under such treatment" (PSG, 2; italics added).

In the second place, the monopolar interpretation forces us into an unattractive dilemma: If one pole of each contrast is regarded as more excellent, so that the supremely excellent being cannot be described by the other and inferior pole, then *either* there is something outside the reality of God, so that the ultimate metaphysical truth is God-and-something-else; *or* (if we would preserve the insight that deity is the all-inclusive being) the "inferior" pole is an illusory reality.

In the third place, experience does not lend support to the idea of monopolarity. Consider the polarity, unity-variety. Is it so obvious that unity is simply superior to variety? True, we may consider it a defect that a person "has too many irons in the fire" and so fails to integrate sufficiently his many interests. But it is equally true that we regard as dull people who integrate too few interests or concerns. Monotony or triviality is in principle as serious a defect as chaos or discord. What we seek in perfection, therefore, is supreme unity in variety: "The ultimate being must fulfill two requirements. It must include all actual states...and yet it must preserve its own identity in the midst of all this diversity of determination."[8]

The conclusion from these considerations "is that the contrast excellent-inferior, the truly invidious contrast, has no tendency to coincide with that between...polar contrasts...but, rather, this invidious contrast breaks out indifferently on both sides of the categorial polarities" (PSG, 4). There are superior and inferior forms of variety and complexity, but likewise superior and inferior forms of unity. *Both* sides of the categorial contraries admit a superior or supreme case, or "supercase" (PSG, 5). Rather than saying, then, that God's perfection consists in his including one, "superior," pole and excluding the other, "inferior," pole, should we not say that God is the superior form of both poles of each contrast?

The insight that we must protect is that God's perfection is definable conceptually and not merely factually, for he surpasses not only every actual creature, but every creature that is so much as even *possible*. God is not merely a very good, or even the most good, being. His surpassability in goodness is a matter of principle, not merely of degree. "We may call this divergence 'categorical supremacy.' Now our suggestion is that there is a monopolar and a dipolar way of conceiving such supremacy" (PSG, 7).[9] On the dipolar interpretation of categorial supremacy, God's perfection consists, not in his realization of the "superior" pole of each contrast (this interpretation, as we have argued, contradicts both logic and experience), but in his superior realization of both sides of all categorial contrasts. "Eminence is in *how* a being is contingent and how it is independent or necessary" (CS, 269). Thus God is supremely absolute and supremely related to all, the supreme form of being as well as the supreme form of becoming, the cause of which all else is effect, as well as the effect of which all else is cause.

These predications are not contradictory, because they are made of different aspects of the divine nature, and "there is no law of logic against attributing contrasting predicates to the same individual, provided they apply to diverse aspects of this individual" (PSG, 14-15). The diverse aspects are, of course, abstract existence and concrete actuality. "The two sides of the transcendent duality are...reconciled by the old principle that the concrete contains the abstract" (CS, 236-37). Thus God is eternal, absolute, necessary in his essence-existence, but temporal, relative and contingent in his concrete actuality.

The same arguments which weaken the case for the monopolar conception of the divine attributes strengthen the case in favor of the dipolar interpretation. Thus: (1) dipolarity provides a sound base for a consistent analogous conception of deity. For example, whereas a man, in his abstract identity, is relatively independent--and so exclusive of others, and in his concrete actuality relatively dependent upon and so inclusive of some others; God, in his abstract identity, is supremely absolute and totally independent of the world, and in his concrete fullness supremely related to all and supremely inclusive of world process. The terms "dependent" and "independent" or "inclusive" and "exclusive" save the comparison from equivocation; and the difference between "all" (actual or merely possible) and "some" or between "supremely" and "relatively" prevent its being univocal. (2) The dipolar interpretation allows us to achieve a higher synthesis of classical theism (God is independent of world process) and pantheism (God includes world process). This sheer comprehensiveness, this ability to include without distortion or contradiction the insights of both theism and pantheism while avoiding their paradoxes, is one of the strongest arguments in favor of the "panentheistic" or dipolar conception of God. (3) Finally, dipolarity allows us to preserve our most basic insights and experiences, that, for example, unity is always unity in variety, and necessity always necessity in contingency.

4.3 *Concrete and Abstract Dimensions of Value*

There is yet another puzzle in the classical motif. If God is *actus purus*, and so not subject to increase in any respect, then he must possess (or simply be) the ultimate expression of all value. But the notion of ultimate or maximal value, taken without qualification, is problematic. Some values do not *in principle* admit a maximum or upper limit, so that it makes no sense to speak of God's possessing them in an ultimate way. Knowledge, for example, measured by the richness, variety and harmony of its objects, can have no maximal form. Why? Because it is inherent in the character of reality as the cumulative actualization of possibilities that there will always be *new* actualities for a perfect knower to know. On the other hand, knowledge measured by freedom from error or ignorance can have a maximal expression--namely, complete adequacy to and comprehensiveness of all that is actual as actual, and all that is possible as possible. In short, omniscience as aesthetic *enjoyment* is infinitely perfectible and capable of increase in enrichment, whereas omniscience as *infallible* is absolutely perfect and incapable of increase.

What Hartshorne is pointing out here is the distinction between *concrete* values (love of x, knowledge of y, power over z) and the *abstract* qualities of these values (perfect love, ultimate wisdom, supreme power). Concrete values are an open infinity, whereas the abstract dimensions of value admit a maximal expression. Thus, instead of simply equating God's perfection with an unchanging possession of maximum value, "must we not proceed more cautiously and define 'perfection' rather as the categorically ultimate form of all attributes that admit such form (it can be shown that they are abstract aspects of value) and the categorically superior form of all attributes that do not admit an ultimate form (they are all ways of expressing the concrete value, happiness)? By categorically superior we mean such that no other individual can rival it, thus leaving open the door to self-excelling" (PSG, 10).

It will, I think, be obvious that this distinction between categorial *ultimacy* and categorial *superiority*, or between *perfect* and *perfectible*, rests on exactly the same logical principle as do both the dipolar interpretation of the divine attributes and the distinction between the divine essence-existence and the divine actuality: namely, the principle that *the concrete contains the abstract* and *only* the concrete can embody the abstract, or again, the abstract *is* only as a generic feature of a concrete inclusive whole. "Abstract entities are not real simply in themselves, apart from all concrete embodiment...the basic form of reality is concrete reality...abstract reality is somehow derivative" (CS, 22).

5. Conclusions

In the Introduction I raised the question of divine mystery: is not God the unfathomable mystery who lies beyond the limits of rational inquiry? We are now in a position to give an answer. God *in one respect* utterly transcends metaphysical analysis, and *in another respect* is the very pinnacle of metaphysical knowledge. The neoclassical conception of God does not dissolve the divine mystery, rather it shows precisely (and coherently) where the mystery lies: not in the mere concept or essence of divinity, but in the concrete fullness of the divine actuality. Hartshorne's remarks on this point are self-explanatory: "There is mystery enough about God, not because his eternal 'essence' is inaccessible, ...but because particular actuality, even divine actuality, is not metaphysical but empirical" (NT, 77). Thus "God may be at once the most baffling and the most intelligible of all realities, depending upon whether we have in mind the concrete or the abstract in His reality" (LP, 5). Or again:

> Reason deals with the universal and abstract; the wholly particular and concrete can only be intuited. Thus, in so far as faith, or life-trust, has something particular as its object it transcends rational evidence....Rational theology may be able to show that there is a God who cherishes all his creatures, but no rational discipline can show there is a God who cherishes "me"....That about God which reason cannot know is not the essence of God, that which he is in general terms, such as all-knowing, or loving; but the particular form that this knowing or loving takes when a given particular creature is its object. Not the essence, but the most particular of the accidents of God have to be felt rather than demonstrated, if we can know them at all. (RSP, 171-72)

Once again, we may draw an analogy to the human self: that which is eminently knowable about a person is his or her most abstract features; that which is mysterious or intuited, if at all, only in close friendship is the concrete fullness of the person.

Thus the existence-actuality distinction removes the strongest intuitive objection to the ontological proof: that the complete (and ultimately mysterious) reality of God is

somehow simply deduced from an abstract definition. On Hartshorne's interpretation, what is deduced is very little, but it
is a precious little: not any concrete state of God, but the
bare truth that there must be some state or other. What is
proved to be necessary is not concrete divine actuality but
abstract divine existence, "unlimited power to preserve self-
identity and integrity in response to any world whatever" (AD,
121), the absolutely infinite capacity to survive change, the
"ability to adapt without compromise in essentials" (CS, 232),
the "absolute 'patience' of God for the variety of existence"
(AD, 175-76), "the absolutely infinite range of variability
in...possible hows of actualization" (AD, 301-302). Thus from
an abstract conception we deduce only an equally abstract
truth, the peculiarity of *this* truth being that it not only
does not exclude having contingent exemplifications, but it
requires both that there be exemplifications and that these
exemplifications be contingent states of one individual. Mere
"existing deity" is a concept formally incapable of lacking
actualization. "It is necessary that God be capable of contingent qualifications, and that His capacity for such qualifications be unsurpassable" (AD, 209).

Finally, the importance of the Hartshornean reconception
of perfection as modal coextensiveness can be seen in two ways.
In the first place, it allows us to uphold the Whiteheadian
dictum that "God is not to be treated as an exception to all
metaphysical principles, invoked to save their collapse. He
is their chief exemplification."[10] Thus if reality is creative
process, the actualization of possibility, then the divine
power is to be conceived as "constitutive of possibility itself" (LP, 149) as well as inclusive of actuality. In the
second place, this theistic reconception highlights the intuitive force of the ontological proof. The range of God's existence is strictly coordinate to that of all possible states of
affairs. There is, then, no such possibility as the possibility that God does not exist. The ground of possibility cannot
itself be a mere possibility.

[1]To be sure, I may say that my past history is *conditionally* necessary: given the present state of affairs, it will always be true that I went to such-and-such a grade school, etc. But *that* I should exist at all--then, now, or in the future--remains radically contingent. That is to say, at every moment of my existence there are possible worlds which exclude my existence.

[2]Hartshorne, "The Formal Validity and Real Significance of the Ontological Argument," p. 227.

[3]Hartshorne, "Necessity," p. 295.

[4]Hartshorne uses "modal *coextensiveness*" and "modal *coincidence*" interchangeably. My own preference is for the former, since it avoids any possible pantheistic or monistic overtones which are implied by "coincidence." On at least one occasion Hartshorne has indicated the same preference. Thus, when speaking of God's possibility as "coincidence with possibility as such," he adds in parentheses, "Perhaps 'coextensiveness' with possibility would be more accurate" (LP, 38).

[5]To say that the unrestricted disjunction of all possible states of affairs is infinite is not to deny that at any *given* time not everything is really (or logically) possible. What is really possible at any given time is possible only within the confines of preceding actuality, and so is finite. However, the range of possibilities for *all* times is strictly infinite.

[6]Hartshorne, "Necessity," p. 291.

[7]See Findlay's article, "Can God's Existence Be Disproved?", pp. 47-56.

[8]Hartshorne, "Santayana's Doctrine of Essence," p. 145.

[9]Professor Hartshorne has requested that the "categorical" in "categorical supremacy" (and in all subsequent quotations) should more properly be read as "categorial." "Categorical" carries the strict logical connotation of "non-hypothetical," whereas the intended sense is "absolute" or "unqualified," i.e., *categorial*.

[10]Whitehead, *Process and Reality*, p. 405.

CHAPTER IV

POSSIBILITY AND MODALITY

"To talk about necessary existence is *ipso facto* to enter the realm of modality" (LP, 103). The second major issue involved in Hartshorne's ontological proof is his theory of modality, and here--as in the theory of divinity--the interpretive key is the metaphysics of temporal possibility. By a "theory of modality" I mean a set of arguments concerning the nature of logical possibility and necessity, ontological possibility and necessity, and the relation between the two. Hartshorne, for example, contends that his proof deduces not only the logical necessity, but also the ontological necessity of the divine existence: "To say that the proposition affirming the divine existence is *logically* necessary not only does not contradict, but on my theory entails, that the existence itself is really necessary (could not have failed to be)."[1]

The technical terms for logical and ontological modalities are modality *de dicto* and modality *de re*. By *de dicto* modality we mean the predication of a modal property (necessity or contingency) of another dictum or proposition, for example, "Necessarily, God exists," which means that "God exists" is a logically necessary truth. By *de re* modality we mean the predication of a necessary or accidental property of some object or individual, for example, "God exists necessarily," which says that God has the (ontologically) essential property of necessary existence. *De dicto* modalities thus express logical or linguistic properties, whereas *de re* modalities express ontological or real properties. Symbolically, the two modalities can be expressed thus: $\Box(x)(Fx{\supset}Gx)$ or $\Diamond(x)(Fx{\supset}Gx)$ (*de dicto*), and $(x)(Fx{\supset}\Box Gx)$ or $(x)(Fx{\supset}\Diamond Gx)$ (*de re*). Formally, then, the distinction is that in cases of *de dicto* modality, the modal operator ($\Box$ or $\Diamond$) falls *outside* the scope of the (universal or existential) quantifier, whereas in cases of *de re* modality, the modal operator falls *within* the scope of the quantifier.

Hartshorne's modal theory revolves around his contention that in the ontological proof modality *de dicto* and modality

de re are coextensive and even inseparable: "What I try to do
is to present a theory of the *inseparability* of the two kinds
of necessity, an inseparability which the Proof tends to show."[2]
Or again: "Where necessity is meant, as the Proof intends, unconditionally, there the *de re* and *de dicto* forms of necessity
should be taken as coextensive" (AD, 115).

The modal aspect of Hartshorne's ontological proof has
been subjected to three principal criticisms: (1) contemporary
logic will not permit the necessary existential statement which
lies at the foundation of Hartshorne's proof; (2) the distinction between *de dicto* necessity and *de re* necessity cannot be
collapsed; consequently, if Hartshorne claims to prove both the
logical and the ontological necessity of God's existence,
either his proof equivocates in the use of "necessity," *or* (if
the proof is to be interpreted consistently in terms of logical
necessity) the argument has no ontological relevance whatsoever; (3) the concept of *de re* necessity is meaningless, so
that while we may speak of the logical necessity of God's existence, talk about the ontologically necessary existence of God
is a philosophical muddle. (1) challenges whether any exis-
tence--even the divine--can be logically necessary; (2) and (3)
grant the logical necessity, but challenge Hartshorne's claim
that the logical necessity of the divine existence warrants the
ontological necessity of that existence. My thesis in this
chapter is that Hartshorne's metaphysics of temporal possibility provides the resources for answering all three criticisms.

1. Necessary Existential Statements

To begin with (1): this objection comes from John Hick,
who contends that the first premise of Hartshorne's proof,
$(\exists x)(Px) \rightarrow \Box(\exists x)(Px)$, combines the two notions of logical necessity and existence, and so is outside one of the cardinal
canons of modern logic. This objection, of course, has deep
philosophical roots which go back to Hume's strict separation
of necessary, analytic, *a priori*, non-existential propositions
from contingent, synthetic, *a posteriori*, existential propositions. "One cannot treat an existential proposition as a
logically necessary truth."[3]

Why not? "Necessarily, something exists" is both a necessary proposition, and a proposition about existence (see Chapter II, section 1.3). What could falsify this proposition? Only non-existence. But refutation by non-existing evidence is just non-refutation. What law is Hick appealing to here? Will he deny that $\Box(\exists x)(x>7)$ is a necessary proposition containing an existential quantifier? Certainly there is no law of logic to justify Hick's assertion.

Hick's point, it would seem, is rather the philosophical one that existential status can never be logically necessary. Put this way, however, the point is question-begging, because Hartshorne's argument is that while *actuality* can in no case be logically necessary, the class of contingent actualities can-- in the unique divine case--be *necessarily* non-empty, and this can be shown to be a *logical* truth (see Chapter III, 4.1). "Existence is always arbitrary selection or determination among the possible values of a variable x in $(\exists x)fx$. Ordinarily, however, the possibilities include the vacuous case of no value. In necessary existence, $N(\exists x)fx$, the x is still a variable with a range of possible values; however, the vacuous case of no value, $\sim\exists x)fx$, is here *logically* excluded" (LP, 64; italics added).

2. The Connection Between *De Dicto* and *De Re*

In a second and related objection, Hick argues that the success of Hartshorne's proof must depend upon an equivocal use of "necessity." Building on his previous contention that Hartshorne's first premise "does not conform to any propositional form recognized in standard logical theory,"[4] Hick argues that Anselm's Principle must be interpreted as signifying ontological, rather than logical, necessity: if Perfection exists, it exists eternally and *a se*. When the necessity operator is so interpreted, says Hick, proposition 1 constitutes an acceptable premise and leads by valid steps to proposition 6 (for Hartshorne's proof, see above, Chapter I, section 1). However, if we interpret Hartshorne's sixth premise, $Nq \lor N\sim q$, in terms of *ontological* necessity, according to which the divine existence is (ontologically) either necessary or impossible, we cannot (argues Hick) deduce God's existence. "What we can deduce is that *if* there is a God, he has onto-logically necessary (i.e., eternal and self-existent) being."[5] In order to proceed beyond proposition 6, we must interpret N as signifying *logical*, rather than ontological, necessity, so that God's existence is either logically necessary or logically impossible. "We can then argue, as Hartshorne does, that it has not been shown that the existence of God is logically im-possible, and hence that it must be regarded as logically necessary."[6] But this switch in meaning from ontological necessity to logical necessity in proposition 6 is illicit: "the argument, having established prop. 6 in terms of ontologi-cal necessity, must thenceforth proceed on the (false) assump-tion that prop. 6 has been established in terms of logical necessity; and...the proof is rendered invalid by this change of meaning of a key term in midcourse."[7]

In short, Hick's objection is that Hartshorne's proof cannot reach its conclusion *except* by interpreting the neces-sity operator in proposition 6 to signify both logical and ontological necessity. But this "illicit shift of meaning be-tween logical and ontological necessity" fatally disrupts the proof, because "logical necessity is not a case of ontological necessity, nor vice versa."[8]

A variation on this theme of the irreducible distinction between logical necessity and ontological necessity is provided by another critic, W. Donald Hudson, who argues that "talk of necessary existence or non-existence...i.e., *logically* neces-sary existence or non-existence--still tells us nothing about objective, i.e., extra-conceptual, extra-linguistic, reality."[9] Hartshorne is accused of "sliding over the point...that logical implications are one thing, ontological realities another."[10]

Several points are in order here: (1) In the first place, as we argued above (in section 1), it is simply false that Hartshorne's first premise "does not conform to any proposi-tional form recognized in standard logical theory."[11] $\Box(\exists x)Px$ is of exactly the same logical form as $\Box(\exists x)(x>7)$. (2) There-fore, Hartshorne does not "equivocate" in his use of "necessity." "From beginning to end of the formal proof, 'N' stands for

necessity of propositions, and no shift of meaning in this
respect figures in the deductive procedure."[12]

Nevertheless (3), to conclude that God exists (step 10,
$(\exists x)Px$) because the existence of God is *logically* necessary
(step 8, $\Box(\exists x)Px$), "not only does not contradict, but on my
theory entails, that the existence itself is really necessary."[13]
So--contra both Hick and Hudson--Hartshorne insists that an
argument which proves the logical necessity of the divine existence is *ipso facto* an argument which proves ontologically
necessary existence as well. "Propositional necessity mirrors
objective necessity."[14] Thus Hartshorne writes: "As for the
danger of equivocation in the proof between linguistic and
extralinguistic senses of the modal terms, my view would be
that since the objective modalities are reflected in a properly
constructed language, there is nothing necessarily fallacious
in using both the linguistic and the ontological interpretations, provided this is done consistently and the formal reasoning stands up on its own grounds."[15] That "linguistic" and
"extralinguistic" refer, respectively, to modality *de dicto*
and modality *de re* is evidenced by Hartshorne's statement elsewhere that "where necessity is meant, as the Proof intends, unconditionally, there the *de re* and *de dicto* forms of necessity
should be taken as coextensive" (AD, 115). So Hartshorne's
contention is that his argument does not prove "mere" logical
necessity, for the necessity operator in that proof admits both
a *de dicto* and a *de re* interpretation. This doctrine of modal
correspondence is the center of Hartshorne's modal theory.

The roots for Hartshorne's insistence that modality *de
dicto* and modality *de re* are coextensive in his proof lie in
his metaphysics of temporal possibility. *The principles that
modality is essentially temporal, so that possibility, as
futurity, is a metaphysical horizon of preceding actuality, and
that necessity is an abstract feature of all future or once-
future states of affairs, provide the basis for Hartshorne's
theory of modality*. What is logically possible is, by definition, "possible" only as a future outcome of the present state
of world process (or as a once-future outcome of a past stage
of world process). "The potential is an aspect of the existent,

or it is nothing identifiable" (MVG, 257). There is for Hartshorne, then, no such entity as a *mere* logical possibility, if
this means a state of affairs which is logically possible, but
never could really obtain.

> One can still distinguish between what is logically
> as well as really possible, on the one hand, and
> what is 'only logically possible,' on the other--
> provided one means by the latter either that the
> time when the thing in question was still really
> possible lies so remotely in our past, or that the
> time when its future real possibility can become
> imminent lies so far off in our future, that it is
> of no relevance to ordinary purposes....In such
> cases it may be convenient to consider the possi-
> bility as though it were *merely* logical. But, on
> my view, this is never strictly correct. And in
> some contexts, especially philosophical ones, it
> is by no means safe to forget the principle that
> any possibility is at some time real and future.[16]

If logical possibilities are thus causally related to real
capacities of world process, and if absolute necessity is an
abstract feature pervasive of all possibility, then a logically
necessary proposition, such as "God exists," *must* refer to an
ontologically necessary feature of reality, that is, to an ontological feature of process *qua* process. If there cannot be,
strictly speaking, mere logical possibilities, then *a fortiori*
there cannot be mere logical necessities. "If 'strictly in
terms of logical necessity' is intended to mean, 'not in any
way implying ontological necessity,' then my comment is that
there is and can be no such *merely* logical necessity--except
that of the conditional, or if-then, kind, which is not what
the 'N' is used to symbolize in the proof."[17] Logical modalities refer either to a real capacity of world process (possibility) or to the ultimate *identity* in world process (necessity). "Not that all thought represents actualities, that is,
fully actualized possibilities; rather all thought, not absurd
or inconsistent, represents *either* something necessary, which
never was merely future, *or* something contingent that once was
future."[18]

Consequently (4), Hartshorne takes issue with Hick's contention that if step 6, Nq v N~q, *were* to be interpreted in terms
of ontological necessity, we would be able to deduce only that

if there is a God, he has ontologically necessary being. "If" means "upon some condition," and therefore should be used only in reference to *possibilities* whose actualization is contingent--i.e., might obtain or might not obtain. Unconditional ontological necessity, being on both sides of every contingent alternative, is that which is ingredient in every conceivable world state. What, therefore, can "if" mean in such a context? Upon what conditions might absolute necessity depend?

> Hence I do not see that *a se esse* is intelligible if it allows the *esse* to be properly assertible in a contingent proposition. Here we would have either an objective necessity not mirrored in language (in which case I say we would have a bad language), or else not even an objective necessity. Self-sufficiency and non-contingency (real and logical, both) belong together, not apart. Their mutual independence is an assumption of my critic [Hick]. His view seems to be that while God's existence is not contingent *upon* anything, still it is contingent, i.e., it might not have been....I regard any such divorce of contingency from conditionedness as a mistake.[19]

3. The Intelligibility of *De Re* Modality

Hartshorne's insistence that modality *de dicto* and modality *de re* are coextensive in the ontological proof, so that the necessity operator may be interpreted as expressing either logical or ontological necessity, may provide a sound response to Hick's and Hudson's assumption of the radical disconnectedness of the two modalities; but the very same contention may be subject to severe criticism from another quarter. Almost a decade prior to the publication of the formalized version of Hartshorne's argument in 1962, W. V. O. Quine published his article on "Reference and Modality," in which he launched--in the form of a challenge to quantified modal logic--a serious attack on the whole notion of *de re* modality. Quine's argument was that the concept of necessary properties is a confused, and hence meaningless, notion. Such an argument, if effectively sustained, would undercut Hartshorne's insistence that the ontological argument proves, as well as the logical necessity of the divine existence, that God has the essential property of necessary existence. I regard this attack on the intelligibility

of *de re* modality as the most serious of the objections con-
fronting Hartshorne's modal theory; consequently, I will spend
the remainder of this chapter on an analysis of Quine's argument and on a rebuttal based on principles drawn from Hartshorne's metaphysics of temporal possibility.

3.1 *Quine: the Logical Difficulties Attending Quantified Modal Logic*

Our entry point into the subject of *de re* modality is
quantified modal logic. "Quantified modal logic" refers to
systems of modal logic involving quantification across modal
operators, for example, (∃x) (necessarily, x is greater than
seven). In "Reference and Modality," Quine mounts an attack
on quantified modal logic, an attack which centers around the
three interrelated notions of quantification, singular reference, and substitutivity.

Quine wants to establish the general thesis that quantification into a modal context is nonsensical. For illustration
he chooses the example of existential quantification into a
necessity context. He argues that from the true statement

(1) Necessarily, 9 is greater than 7

we cannot by existential generalization infer

(2) (∃x) (necessarily, x is greater than 7).

Why is it that (1) is not subject to existential generalization? The existential generalization of a sentence says that
something has the property which that sentence predicates of
the denotation of its singular term. The crucial concept here
is *denotation*, or naming. When the singular term in question
fails to denote, existential generalization breaks down.
Linsky writes, "'(∃x)F(x)' is true if and only if there is at
least one object in the domain of discourse that satisfies the
open sentence 'F(x)'....Failure of the inference from 'F(a)' to
'(∃x)F(x)' occurs if and only if 'a' fails of singular reference
in 'F(a)'."[20] Thus, there is a connection between singular
reference and quantification, such that where a singular term
fails to name, we cannot perform existential generalization.
Says Quine: "The idea behind such inference is that whatever is

true of the object named by a singular term is true of something; and clearly the inference loses its justification when
the singular term in question does not happen to name."[21]

So the reason that we cannot perform existential generalization over (1), Quine contends, is that "9" somehow fails to
name or to denote in (1). In Quine's words, "9" has a *referentially opaque* occurrence in (1). We can grasp this notion of
referential opacity by way of example. Consider the statement:

(3) There is no such thing as Pegasus.

It is blatantly wrong to infer from (3) that

(4) $(\exists x)$ (there is no such thing as x).

(4) can be read: "there is something such that it is not." The
reason for this mistake is clear: "Pegasus" does not name anything, it does not refer to anything or denote anything. Its
occurrence in (3) is thus referentially opaque. Or again, consider

(5) 'Cicero' contains six letters.

From (5) we cannot infer

(6) $(\exists x)$ ('x' contains six letters).

"'x' contains six letters" simply means "the 24th letter of the
alphabet contains six letters." Thus, as Plantinga writes, (6)
represents a "vacuous quantification of an outrageous false-
hood."[22] Obviously the problem here is that 'Cicero' in (5)
does not have its usual reference; it does not refer to the *man*
Cicero, but to the *word* "Cicero." So 'Cicero' has a referentially opaque occurrence in (5).

A singular term thus has a referentially opaque occurrence
when it fails to denote or when it has other than its usual
denotation. Sentences in which referential opacity occurs are
called by Quine "referentially opaque contexts," and it is in
these contexts that existential generalization fails. Examples
of referentially opaque contexts are "believes that...," "is
unaware that...," and the context of singular quotes.

Now Quine's argument is that the modal operators provide
another case of referentially opaque contexts. That is,

(1) $\Box(9>7)$

resembles

(5) 'Cicero' contains six letters

in just this respect: that neither "9" nor 'Cicero' has purely referential occurrence.

But what is the test for referential occurrence? That is, how can we know when a term occurs in a purely referential or in a referentially opaque context? Quine's criterion for referential occurrence is, in a word, *substitutivity*, or Leibniz's law of the indiscernibility of identicals. The law says that "*given a true statement of identity, one of its two terms may be substituted for the other in any true statement and the result will be true.*"[23] Examples of identity statements are

(7) Cicero = Tully

and

(8) 9 = the number of the planets.

Just as there is an intimate connection between quantification and reference, so there is a close tie between reference and substitutivity. As Linsky writes, "that the terms of a true identity statement are everywhere inter-substitutive, *salva veritate*, is merely explicative of the idea of singular terms' having singular reference."[24] In other words, since the terms of a true identity statement refer to the same object, in any true sentence we should be able to replace one term by the other and leave the truth value of the original sentence unchanged--provided the two terms have referential occurrence. For example, both

(9) Cicero denounced Cataline

and

(10) Tully denounced Cataline

are true because Cicero = Tully *and* because "Cicero" and "Tully" both have referential occurrence. On the other hand, although

(5) 'Cicero' contains six letters

is true,

(11) 'Tully' contains six letters

is false. What is the problem here? Obviously, we cannot invoke the identity

(7) Cicero = Tully

because 'Cicero' and 'Tully' occur in referentially opaque contexts in (5) and (11). That is, *referential opacity causes failure of substitutivity*: this is Quine's rule.

In short, the indiscernibility of identicals provides Quine with a criterion for determining when singular terms have referential occurrence and when they do not: if substitutivity fails, then the original context is referentially opaque. Using this criterion, Quine argues that modal contexts induce referential opacity precisely because they produce failure of substitutivity. That is,

(1) $\Box(9>7)$

is not by

(8) 9 = the number of the planets

equivalent to

(12) $\Box$(the number of planets>7),

and thus in (1) "9" does not have referential occurrence. We know that "9" does not have referential occurrence in (1) because when we substitute "the number of planets" for "9" we change a true statement (1) into the false statement (12). Substitutivity breaks down. "Since the principle of substitutivity is analytic of the idea of singular reference, we are left with no alternative but to conclude that '9' in 'N(9>7)' does not make singular reference to '9'."[25]

Quine's argument, then, runs as follows: modal contexts produce failure of substitutivity; failure of substitutivity betrays referential opacity; and referential opacity prevents existential generalization. Thus

(1) $\Box(9>7)$

fails of existential generalization. What is the "x" in

(2) $(\exists x)$ (necessarily, x>7)

which is greater than 7? According to (8) it is the number of
the planets, but certainly it is not a necessary truth that the
number of the planets is greater than 7.

In short, although it is a necessary truth that 9 is
greater than 7, it is not a necessary truth that what is identical with 9--the number of the planets--is greater than 7.
Quine concludes that "to be necessarily greater than 7 is not a
trait of a number, but depends on the manner of referring to
the number."[26] Or, more generally, "being necessarily or possibly thus and so is in general not a trait of the object concerned, but depends on the manner of referring to the object."[27]

No doubt, Quine's argument is clever, but is it conclusive?
I think not, for Quine does not prove his conclusion to be unambiguously true. Consider once again the statement that "to
be necessarily greater than 7 is not a trait of a number, but
depends on the manner of referring to the number."[28] Let us
examine both clauses of this claim.

To be necessarily greater than 7 is not a trait of a
number--what exactly does Quine mean here? Alvin Plantinga has
understood Quine to say that

Necessarily, _____ is greater than 7

(where the blank is to be filled in by a singular term) does
not express a trait or property.[29] But precisely why is

(12) □(the number of planets>7)

false? Is it, as Quine suggests, because the modal context,
□(____>7), fails to express a property? Well, this is not obviously the case, because in at least one substitution instance,
namely, □(9>7), "9" expresses the property of being necessarily
greater than 7. Granted, necessary-greaterness-than-7 is not
in all cases a property of the number of planets--yet it is a
property of 9. So some instances of □(____>7) express a property, while others do not.

The interesting question, it seems to me, is where we locate the cause of this problem: in the modal context *per se*, or
in the singular terms chosen for substitution? Now if *all* instances of □(____>7) resulted in false propositions, we would

certainly be justified in concluding that necessary-
greaterness-than-7 does not express a property. But if some
identifiable sector of substitution instances does express the
property, then it seems unfair to conclude that there is no
such property. "Why, after all," asks Plantinga, "should we
suppose that *every* instance of a context expressing a property
P must predicate P of the denotation (if any) of its singular
term? Is it not sufficient that some large and systematically
identifiable range of its instances do so?"[30] One way to identify that sector of substitution instances which do express
properties in modal contexts is to distinguish between proper
names and definite descriptions. We will return to this point
shortly.

Consider now the second part of Quine's conclusion--"but
depends on the manner of referring to the number." This certainly looks like a decisive objection to the notion of *de re*
necessity--but I confess that its purported force eludes me.
As long as we are indeed "referring *to the number*" (Quine's
phrase), then *the number* (the denotation of the singular term)
has the property in question. "Being necessarily greater than
7" expresses a property of 9 whether we refer to 9 as "3^2" or
as "the whole number between 8 and 10" or as "the number of
planets"--*in those cases where "the number of planets" denotes
9*. But--so goes the objection--surely the number of planets
could have been 5. Yes, but if we are specifying *that* counterfactual situation, then we are not referring to 9. How does
this objection upset the thesis that whenever we do refer to 9,
we refer to a number that has the property of "being necessarily greater than 7"? I see nothing puzzling or mysterious
here.

3.2 *The Smullyan Reply*

Thus far I have agreed with Quine that there are logical
problems involved in quantified modal logic, but I have con-
tested his claim that those problems are intrinsic to the modal
contexts, and I have suggested instead that the problems may
trace back to the nature of the singular terms chosen for

substitution. Indeed, Quine's phrase, "singular terms," masks
just the distinction between proper names and definite descriptions which provides the logical machinery for explaining why
definite descriptions cause problems when they are used as substitution instances in modal contexts. All of Quine's arguments against failure of substitutivity in modal contexts, as
Arthur Smullyan has pointed out,[31] depend upon interchanging
definite descriptions for proper names. Now, one of the features distinguishing names from descriptions, on the traditional
Russellian explanation, is that in certain contexts descriptions
induce scope ambiguities, while names do not. Consider Russell's
example:

(13) The present King of France is not bald.

The scope of the definite description is ambiguous here. Do we
mean to say

(13') $[(\imath x)(Kx)]$ $\{\sim B(\imath x)(Kx)\}$

that is, There is an entity which is now King of France and is
not bald; or do we mean

(13") $\sim[(\imath x)(Kx)]$ $\{B(\imath x)(Kx)\}$

that is, It is not the case that there is an entity which is
now King of France and is bald? The ambiguity arises according
to whether the definite description, "the present King of
France," is interpreted as having primary (13') or secondary
(13") occurrence.

On the other hand,

(14) Nixon is not a Democrat

is unambiguous, because "Nixon" is a proper name rather than a
definite description. Consequently, there is no difference in
truth value between "Nixon is not a Democrat" and "It is not
the case that Nixon is a Democrat." Proper names do not induce
scope ambiguities.

(To be sure, Russell himself would not have regarded
"Nixon" as a *logically* proper name, but as an *ordinary* proper
name, and hence a disguised description. This Russellian
practice of treating ordinary proper names as disguised

descriptions is a result of his epistemological doctrine of
knowledge by acquaintance: unless we are acquainted with the
referent of a name, that name for us is a disguised description. However, this epistemological thesis can be separated
from Russell's logical behavior thesis, so that we can uphold
the logical doctrine even if we decide to assimilate ordinary
proper names to logically proper names. In this paper I am
accepting Russell's logical thesis and rejecting his epistemological thesis, and I am adopting, without argument, Kripke's
position that ordinary proper names are to be treated as logically proper names.)

Now Smullyan has simply applied the Russellian logical
behavior thesis to modal contexts. In such contexts definite
descriptions, such as "the number of planets," will induce
scope ambiguities, whereas proper names will not. Thus,

(1) $\Box(9>7)$

is unambiguous, because "9" is a proper name. (1) is analyzed
simply as $\Box Fy$. On the other hand,

(12) $\Box$(the number of planets>7)

is ambiguous. Does the description have primary or secondary
occurrence? That is, does (12) have the form

(12') $[(\imath x)(\emptyset x)] \Box \{F(\imath x)(\emptyset x)\}$

or does it have the form

(12") $\Box\{[(\imath x)(\emptyset x)] F(\imath x)(\emptyset x)\}$?

The import of the distinction becomes clear when we eliminate
the definite description. (12') then becomes

(12a') $(\exists x)$ (x numbers the planets and (y) (if y numbers
the planets, then x=y) and $\Box(x>7)$)

i.e., the number that *in fact* numbers the planets is necessarily greater than 7. And (12") becomes

(12a") $\Box(\exists x)$ (x numbers the planets and (y) (if y numbers
the planets, then x=y) and x>7)

i.e., it is necessary that the number that numbers the planets
is greater than 7. The scope ambiguity thus translates into a

de re-de dicto ambiguity. (12a') is a true statement of *de re* necessity, while (12a") is a false statement of *de dicto* necessity. The point is that the definite description in (12) induces the ambiguity.

Smullyan's criticism of Quine, then, is twofold. (i) Quine ignores Russell's distinction of scope by assuming that (12) must mean (12a"). (ii) The reason that Quine ignores scope distinction is that he ignores the more fundamental distinction between proper names and definite descriptions; he speaks only of the substitutivity of "singular terms," apparently without regard for the fact that "singular terms" cover both names and descriptions. Smullyan's contention is that "the modal paradoxes arise not out of any intrinsic absurdity in the use of the modal operators but rather out of the assumption that descriptive phrases are names."[32] Smullyan's proposal is that only those singular terms in which scope ambiguities do not arise (i.e., proper names) will serve as valid substitution instances in modal contexts. Thus, for example, "the number of the planets" will not serve as an unambiguously valid substitution instance for "9" in "(9>7)"--not because of any paradox intrinsic to the modal context, but because "the number of the planets" is not a proper name.

Thus far we are on purely logical ground: Quine has pointed out the logical problems attending quantified modal logic--referential opacity, failure of substitutivity, failure of existential generalization. Smullyan, on the other hand, has provided a logical explanation for Quine's problem of reference and modality, namely, the logical behavior thesis that names and descriptions perform differently in modal contexts.

Unfortunately, Smullyan's response is not definitive; for in illustrating the logical behavior thesis in modal contexts, Smullyan employs an instance of quantifying into modal contexts (12a'), which is just the practice that Quine has challenged. Of course, we could retort that Quine's challenge depends upon ignoring the distinction between names and descriptions, but then it is equally true that in drawing the distinction Smullyan assumes without argument the intelligibility of quantification across modal operators. We face a logical standoff: Quine

accusing Smullyan of illicit quantification into modal contexts; Smullyan accusing Quine of ignoring the distinction between names and descriptions. Nevertheless, the situation is
instructive in that it indicates what an effective response to
Quine's position must entail, namely, a *semantics* which gives
an intelligible account of quantification into modal contexts.

Quine himself provides the best evidence that the solution
to his problem will have to be semantical. In his response to
Smullyan, Quine does not *deny* that we can distinguish between
names and descriptions; rather, he argues that we have to pay
too high a price to maintain the distinction. Drawing the distinction between names and descriptions involves "adopting an
invidious attitude toward certain ways of uniquely specifying
x,...and favoring other ways...as somehow better revealing the
'essence' of the object."[33] His final decision is that a "re-
version to Aristotelian essentialism is required if quantification into modal contexts is to be insisted on."[34] "Aristotelian essentialism" is understood as the doctrine that "an object,
of itself and by whatever name or none, must be seen as having
some of its traits necessarily and others contingently."[35]

What needs to be emphasized is why Quine's problem is
semantical. Essentialism is simply meaningless to Quine, because predicating necessity of objects is at odds with the
understanding of necessity as analytic. Says Quine: "The general idea of strict modalities is based on the putative notion
of analyticity as follows: a statement of the form
'Necessarily...' is true if and only if the component statement
which 'necessarily' governs is analytic."[36] So it is built
into the very meaning of "analytic" that "necessity" refers to
a certain way of specifying an object, not to an object itself.
Quine's example is that

(Quine's 32) $x = \sqrt{x} + \sqrt{x} + \sqrt{x} \neq \sqrt{x}$

and

(Quine's 33)   There are exactly x planets

both uniquely specify x, but (32) has "x>7" as a necessary consequence, while (33) does not. "*Necessary* greaterness than 7

makes no sense as applied to a *number* x; necessity attaches
only to the connection between 'x>7' and the particular method
(32), as opposed to (33), of specifying x."[37]

Quine's point here is crucial: *given only a* de dicto
understanding of necessity, an understanding that predicates
necessity of analytic propositions, we do not know what
$(\exists x)\Box(x>7)$ *means.* What proposition is it that "$\Box$" governs
here? The symbol "$\Box$" has been defined as "a (monadic)
proposition-forming operator on propositions."[38] But "x>7" is
not a proposition, because it is incapable of being true or
false; it is, rather, a propositional function. So far Quine
is entirely right: we do not have a semantical meaning for
"$\Box(x>7)$"--hence it is meaningless.

Quine's attack, in short, issues at the semantical level.
"It is modal logic as *interpreted* that draws his fire."[39]
Clearly what we require as a response to Quine is a semantics
for quantified modal logic. We need to state intelligibly what
the truth conditions for $(\exists x)\Box(x>7)$ are. Linsky writes: "It is
apparent that what is required in order to defeat Quine's challenge (not argument) is a clear semantics for quantified modal
logic."[40]

3.3 *Modality* De Re *and Hartshorne's Argument*

We may pause at this point to ask precisely how Quine's
attack relates to Hartshorne's proof. It is to be noted at the
outset that Quine and Hartshorne have never addressed one
another on this issue of the intelligibility of *de re* modality
and its relevance to the ontological argument. I am therefore
applying Quine's objection to Hartshorne's proof, and then employing Hartshornean principles to respond to Quine. I regard
this effort to narrow the gap between logician and metaphysi-
cian as the specifically constructive feature of the study.

Intuitively speaking, the relevance of Quine's attack to
Hartshorne's argument is this: the very concept of essential
properties is under attack, and *ipso facto* Hartshorne's insistence that the ontological argument proves not only the logical,
but also the ontological necessity of God's existence (i.e., not

only is "God exists" logically necessary, but also God has the
essential property of necessary existence) is also under attack. Formally speaking, if necessary existence is analytic
of the idea of Perfection (and this is just the point of Anselm's discovery), then Hartshorne is committed not only to
the proposition, $\Box(\exists x)Px$, but also to the proposition, $(\exists x)\Box Px$,
that is, he is committed both to "Necessarily, Perfection ex-
ists," and to "There is a being which is necessarily perfect."
And the latter proposition employs quantification across a
modal operator, which is just the practice that initiated
Quine's attack.

It is to be pointed out that Hartshorne has never actually
employed the proposition, $(\exists x)\Box Px$. But, not only has he never
denied the proposition, the whole logic of his theory of modal
correspondence indicates that he *must* affirm the proposition.
The following is used as evidence to support this contention:

(1) At least one of Hartshorne's critics has urged Quine's
argument against him, thereby assuming that Hartshorne affirms
the proposition, $(\exists x)\Box Px$. David Braine writes:

> Hartshorne never so much as touches on how the argu-
> ment might be affected by the problems of intension-
> ality. He holds that the necessity of God's existence
> is *de re* (i.e., necessary existence is a property),
> as well as *de dictu*...and the arguments he and Malcolm
> recommend do indeed depend on this....Yet, if "God
> necessarily exists" expresses a *de re* necessity,
> then the term "God" occurs extensionally and its
> context is free of referential opacity.[41]

Braine goes on to argue that the term "God" is *not* free of
referential opacity (and therefore the necessity of God's existence is not *de re*), for obviously such propositions as "He
whom John Smith worships necessarily exists" (this being a
proposition got by substituting a definite description contingently true of God for the term "God") are not true. John
Smith may in fact worship one of his ancestors or Rosemary's
baby. Braine's objection is Quinean through and through: his
point is that if the necessity of God's existence were *de re*,
then God (by whatever name or none) would have the *property* of
necessary existence. "God" therefore should not have a referentially opaque occurrence. But "God" *does* have a referentially

opaque occurrence; therefore, the necessity of God's existence is not *de re*, but is a linguistic truth which depends upon how we refer to God.

The plausibility of Braine's attack depends upon his contention that Hartshorne is committed to the *de re* (as well as the *de dicto*) interpretation of the divine necessity; and there is only one way to formalize this contention: Hartshorne *must* be committed to the proposition, $(\exists x)\Box Px$.

(2) Hartshorne's own comments regarding *de dicto* necessity and *de re* necessity in the proof leave no doubt that he is solidly committed to both interpretations of the divine necessity. Thus he says that "the *de re* and the *de dicto* forms of necessity should be taken as coextensive" in the proof (AD, 115), and he speaks of "the *inseparability* of the two kinds of necessity."[42] Thus, even though the necessity operator in his argument "means analytic or L-true, true by necessity of the meanings of the terms employed" (LP, 53), Hartshorne insists elsewhere that the proof can be given both an ontological and a linguistic interpretation.[43] Finally, Hartshorne writes, "to say that the proposition affirming the divine existence is *logically* necessary not only does not contradict, but on my theory entails, that the existence itself is really necessary";[44] and when this statement is taken in conjunction with the contention that *de dicto* and *de re* necessity are coextensive, I see--by the meaning of "*de re*," "*de dicto*," and "entails"--no other choice but that Hartshorne is committed to the proposition, $\Box (\exists x)Px . \supset . (\exists x)\Box Px$.

(3) Hughes and Creswell refer to G. H. von Wright's "Principle of Predication," according to which

> all properties can be divided into two types: (a) those whose belonging to an object is always either necessary or impossible, and which we may call *formal* properties; and (b) those whose belonging to an object is always contingent, never a matter of necessity or impossibility, and which we may call *material* properties. If $\emptyset$ is a formal property we therefore have: $(x)(L\emptyset x \vee L\backsim\emptyset x)$; and if $\emptyset$ is a material property we have: $(x)(M\emptyset x \cdot M\backsim\emptyset x)$.[45]

Now this distinction between properties whose instantiation is contingent and properties whose instantiation is necessary is operative in Hartshorne's thought. Examples of the first type are "red," "tall," "two-legged," etc.; and examples of the second are "omniscient," "infallible," and, especially, "perfect." Whereas "red hair," for example, may or may not be exemplified by an individual, it is not so with "perfect": "A perfection exemplified merely contingently would be exemplified by something imperfect, hence not exemplified" (LP, 103). Therefore, "Perfection cannot be of one type with ordinary predicates" (LP, 31), because its belonging to an object is either necessary or impossible. In von Wright's terminology, perfection would be a *formal* property. Hartshorne is thus committed to the proposition that every individual is either necessarily perfect or necessarily not perfect, or, symbolically, (x)($\Box$Px v $\Box$∿Px)--and this proposition involves quantification across modal operators. "Necessity can perfectly well relate the concept 'perfection' to the concept 'necessarily exemplified property'" (LP, 92).

My conclusion from examination of this evidence is that, although Hartshorne has never explicitly employed quantification across modal contexts, the logic of his modal theory commits him to two instances of quantified modal logic: ($\exists$x)$\Box$Px and (x)($\Box$Px v $\Box$∿Px). The tenability of his theory of modal correspondence in the ontological proof, therefore, depends upon an effective resolution of Quine's problem. Note: I am not arguing that Hartshorne's proof depends upon a defense of *de re* necessity when the necessity operator in that proof is interpreted strictly in terms of *de dicto* necessity; I am claiming, however, that Hartshorne's contentions that the proof can be given a *de re* interpretation and that it proves that God has the essential property of necessary existence do depend upon such a defense.

3.4 *Kripke Semantics*

We interrupted our investigation of Quine's attack on quantified modal logic (to show how Hartshorne's interpretation of the ontological proof must be involved in that attack) at the point of requiring a clear semantics for quantified modal logic.

The needed semantical framework for quantified modal logic was provided by Saul Kripke in "Semantical Considerations on Modal Logic," (1963).[46] The pure semantics employs the notion of a model structure (m.s.), a model, a quantificational model structure (q.m.s.), and a quantificational model. Kripke's applied semantics exploits Leibniz's notion of "possible worlds." What follows is a technical exposition of Kripke semantics.

For modal *propositional* calculus, we begin with the notion of a model structure, an ordered triple (G,K,R), where K is the set {G,H}, R is a reflexive relation on K, and G is a privileged member of K (G $\neq$ H). Intuitively, says Kripke, "K is the set of all 'possible worlds'; G is the 'real world'. If H_1 and H_2 are two worlds, $H_1 R H_2$ means intuitively that H_2 is 'possible relative to' H_1; i.e., that every proposition *true* in H_2 is *possible* in H_1."[47]

A *model* simply assigns a truth-value to each propositional variable in each world. "Formally, a *model* $\emptyset$ on a m.s. (G,K,R) is a binary function $\emptyset$ (P,H), where P varies over atomic formulae and H varies over elements of K, whose range is the set {T,F}."[48] Definition of the primitive symbols, $\wedge$, $\sim$, $\square$, allows us to build up complex formulae, and to assign truth values to them. For example, $\emptyset$ ($\square$A,H) = T iff $\emptyset$ (A,H') = T for every H'$\in$K such that HRH'; otherwise, $\emptyset$ ($\square$A,H) = F. Intuitively this says that the proposition A is necessary in some world if and only if A is true in all worlds possible relative to H. Or, in brief, a necessarily true proposition is a proposition which is true in every possible world.

For modal *predicate* calculus, we need individual variables, predicate variables and quantifiers. Besides an infinite list of individual variables x, y, z..., we introduce, for each positive integer n, a list of n-adic predicate letters P^n, Q^n,... (we count propositional variables as 0-adic). Thus, by extending the notion of a model structure, we define a quantificational model structure as a model structure (G,K,R) together with a function Ψ which assigns to each member of K a set Ψ(H), called the domain of H. "Intuitively," says Kripke, "Ψ(H) is the set of all individuals existing in H."[49] U is defined as

the set theoretical union of all domains of individuals existing in all possible worlds (intuitively: the sum of all actual
and possible objects), or, formally, $\mathcal{U} = \bigcup_{H \in K} \Psi(H)$.

Now a quantificational model assigns a truth-value to each
propositional variable (P^0, Q^0,...) or to each predicate variable ($P^{n>0}$, $Q^{n>0}$,...) in each possible world. "We define a
quantificational *model* on a q.m.s. (G,K,R) as a binary function
$\emptyset$ (P^n,H), where the first variable ranges over n-adic predicate
letters, for arbitrary n, and H ranges over elements of K."[50]
The case of propositional variables is the same as above:
$\emptyset$ (P^0, H) = T or F. For an atomic formula P^n (x_1,...,x_n),
where n>0, a quantificational model "picks out" of the set
theoretical union of all domains of objects existing in all
possible worlds, those ordered n-tuples which fall under the
extension of P^n, and then assigns a truth value (for a given
assignment (a_1,...,a_n)) to P^n (x_1,...,x_n) in each possible
world. Thus, "we define $\emptyset$ (P^n(x_1,...,x_n), H) = T if the
n-tuple (a_1,...,a_n) is a member of $\emptyset$ (P^n, H); otherwise,
$\emptyset$ (P^n(x_1,...,x_n), H) = F, relative to the given assignment."[51]
We can also assign truth values to complex formulae, using the
propositional connectives $\wedge$, $\sim$, $\square$, as previously defined.

Universal quantification is defined in the following way:
assume that in the formula A(x, y_1,...,y_n) a truth value
$\emptyset$ (A (x, y_1,...,y_n), H) has been assigned for each assignment
to the free variables. Then $\emptyset$ ((x)A(x, y_1,...,y_n), H) = T,
relative to the assignment of b_1,...,b_n to the y_i if and only
if $\emptyset$ (A(x, y_1,...,y_n), H) = T for every assignment of a member
a of Ψ(H) to x. Quantification, then, is only over *existing*
members of $\mathcal{U}$. Kripke's definition of quantification is intended to falsify such inferences as the following: (x)Ax⊃Ay; for
example, "if everything is bald, then the King of France is
bald." The inference is wrong because, although everything in
a certain possible world, H, may have the property A, still, y
may not have it, because y may not exist in H (though it may
exist in some other possible world).

Kripke's rejection of the Barcan formula ((x)□Ax⊃□(x)Ax)
illustrates the semantics. We reject the Barcan formula by
constructing a counter example in which the antecedent is true

and the consequent false. We consider a universe in which there is only the actual world G and one possible world H. In G only one object, a, exists; in H, two objects, a and b, exist. Thus $\Psi(G) = \{a\}$ and $\Psi(H) = \{a,b\}$, where $a \neq b$. Then we define, for a monadic predicate letter, P, a model $\emptyset$, such that the extension of P in G is $\{a\}$, and the extension of P in H is $\{a\}$. Thus $\emptyset(P,G) = \{a\}$ and $\emptyset(P,H) = \{a\}$. Then $\Box Px$ is true in G when x is assigned a; and, since a is the only object in the domain of G, $(x)\Box Px$ is also true in G. (This is the antecedent of the Barcan formula.) But, $(x)Px$ is false in H when x is assigned b (because b falls outside the extension of P in H), and *a fortiori* $\Box(x)Px$ is false in G. (Thus the antecedent of the Barcan formula is true, while the consequent is false, so the formula is rejected.)

Our intuitive interpretation of Kripke's program, then, involves three semantical principles for quantified modal logic: (1) that of individuals existing in different possible worlds. In our example, $a \in \Psi(G)$ and $a \in \Psi(H)$, that is, a exists in the real world and in the world accessible from G. (2) That of individuals falling under the extension of predicates in the various possible worlds. In our example, $\Box Px$ is true in G, under the assignment a, because a falls under the extension of P in G and in H. P is thus an *essential property* of a. (3) That of quantification only over *existing* members of $\mathcal{U}$. Thus, when a quantificational model assigns a truth value to a sentence in a world H, it takes into account only those objects which exist in H. In our example, $(x)\Box Px$ was true in G, under the assignment a, because a and only a exists in G, and because a exists in every world accessible from G.

Using the semantics we can provide a meaning for $(\exists x)\Box(x>7)$. This says that there is some object, x, in this world which has the property, greater-than-7, in this world and in every possible world in which x exists. In other words, x exists in this world and in at least some possible worlds accessible from this world, and x falls under the extension of the predicate, greater-than-7, in every world in which it exists. In this way quantification into the modal context is made intelligible.

3.5 *From Semantics to Metaphysics*

Kripke's semantics for quantified modal logic involves the three ideas of (1) *essential properties*, i.e., those properties which (2) an *individual* possesses in (3) every *possible world* in which it exists. Does the applied semantics answer Quine's challenge? Not quite, because Quine, among others (Hintikka and Chisolm, for example), has argued that there are serious conceptual problems involved in the idea of one and the same individual existing in various possible worlds. These diffi- culties can be summarized as the problem of transworld identity.

What, exactly, is the problem of transworld identity? "Here the claim is that there are deep conceptual difficulties in identifying the same object from world to world--difficul- ties that threaten the very idea of Transworld Identity with incoherence."[52] An example will illustrate the point. Suppose we are considering a possible world in which Nixon lost the 1968 presidential election. Now this possible world is rela- tively easy to understand: it is simply that state of affairs which would have obtained if Nixon had lost the election. But how many--and which--of Nixon's characteristics might we sup- pose to have been otherwise and still be talking about *Nixon*? Surely we can imagine a possible world in which Nixon is not a Republican, but a Democrat, or perhaps even a possible world in which Nixon did not go into politics at all, but is a Soviet scientist. But obviously our "supposing" is becoming more dif- ficult. Is there a possible world in which Nixon is a twelfth- century theologian? Or, to put the question another way, what are the *essential properties* which Nixon must possess (to be Nixon) in every possible world in which he exists? How can we *identify* Nixon, pick him out, locate him in other possible worlds? We are, it seems, hard-pressed to provide answers to these questions. "But if we cannot identify him in W_1, so the argument continues, then we really do not understand the asser- tion that he exists there."[53]

As a result of this problem of transworld identity, Quine argues that "Kaplan and I see eye to eye, negatively, on essen- tialism as applied to particulars. The result is that we can make little sense of identification of particulars across possible worlds. And the result of that is that we can make little sense of quantifying into necessity contexts when the values of the variables are particulars."[54] In a similar vein, Hintikka concludes that "this problem of cross-identification is unsolvable in the case of logical modalities, and Quine is therefore right in this favorite case of his."[55]

There can be no doubt, it seems to me, that Quine's claim that quantified modal logic is committed to essentialism has been vindicated. The introduction of Kripke semantics shows quite clearly that quantification into modal contexts involves the notion of essential properties. But must we, because of the apparent difficulty of identifying or specifying essential properties, take the final step and conclude with Quine, "so much the worse for quantified modal logic"?[56] I think not, because, as I will argue, essentialism need not mean *Aristotelian* essentialism. Hartshorne's process metaphysics provides a genuinely new and coherent way to understand essentialism, and this new understanding provides an intelligible way to unravel the transworld identity knot.

Just as previously we faced the challenge of providing an intelligible semantical account for quantified modal logic, so now we face the challenge of providing an intelligible explanation of our semantics. The issues have undergone reformulation. No longer are we asking why some singular terms fail to have referential occurrence in necessity contexts; for, armed with Kripke's explanation, we can answer that only a proper name designates the same object across possible worlds, whereas descriptions designate different objects from possible world to possible world. And by "the same object" we mean an object having such and such an essential property (or properties) in every world in which it exists or could exist. Now, however, we are asking how we can *identify* one and the same object in different worlds. We are asking for a clear interpretation of what essential properties are, and how we can use them for transworld identification. And, as Linsky contends, this "is not a logical problem but a metaphysical one."[57] What began as a logical puzzle has become, at the hands of semantical analysis, a specifically metaphysical issue, requiring a metaphysical solution.

I consider this an extremely instructive point: the *de re* issue can be viewed, finally, precisely as a metaphysical issue, not according to any extrinsic invasion of metaphysics into logic, but according to the intrinsic dynamics of contemporary philosophical logic itself. Quine's attack is, in the end, a metaphysical challenge. Furthermore, it can be constructively argued that, in this context of the need for a clear and explicit understanding of a semantics for quantified modal logic, Hartshorne's metaphysics can provide a response worthy of critical attention. In process terms, the otherwise formidable problem of transworld identity becomes a question of determining the principle according to which we may ascertain which alternative future states could serve to concretize this particular abstract individual identity. Hartshorne's process philosophy thus provides resources for resolving the transworld identity problem that are significantly different from the resources available to one (such as Quine) who assumes that transworld identity is inextricably tied to an Aristotelian substance metaphysics. In other words, the notion of transworld identity (I will argue) is not unintelligible in itself, but becomes so in the context of a substance metaphysics. I turn now to the substantiation of this thesis.

3.5.1 Possible Worlds

The first step in resolving the transworld identity problem is the realization that it is really a combination of three problems: (1) possible worlds (what are they?), (2) personal or individual identity (what is it?), and (3) essential properties (what are they?). We may begin with the notion of possible worlds.

Kripke has pointed out that the question, How do we locate or pick out or identify an individual in another possible world?, betrays a false picture image of possible worlds. It suggests that possible worlds are *places*, like foreign countries, and that we are to inspect these places--as if through a powerful telescope--in order to identify a certain individual. But, as Kripke argues, "'possible worlds' are *stipulated*, not

discovered by powerful telescopes."[58] He suggests that "counterfactual situation" or "possible state of the world"[59] better
accord with this notion of stipulation.

"Counterfactuals" and "possible world states" are valuable
clues, because they involve the notion of *temporality*. A counterfactual is something that might have been different at an
earlier time (Nixon might have lost the '68 election), and a
possible state of the world carries the idea of a future outcome of present events. In fact, an explanation of possible
worlds in terms of temporality will provide an adequate and
intelligible metaphysical underpinning for quantified modal
logic.

Arthur Prior, for example, suggests:

> we might say that a possible world is (i) one of the
> alternative possible future outcomes of the present
> actual state of affairs; or by a natural extension
> (ii) anything that *was* a possible world in the pre-
> ceding sense, i.e., an outcome of some *past* state
> of affairs which *was* possible at the time, though
> by now it may have been excluded by what has actually
> taken place instead. Or finally, (iii) we may use
> the phrase for anything that constitutes a 'possible
> world' in sense (i) or (ii), together with its past,
> so that a possible world in this last sense is a
> *total course of events* which either is now possible
> or was possible once.[60]

Now the advantage of Hartshorne's philosophy at just this
point is obvious: it provides a full metaphysical underpinning
for a temporal interpretation of possible worlds. The three
principles, (1) that time is objective modality, (2) that possibility is a metaphysical feature of actuality, or pastness,
in its character as destined to be included in some future
reality, and (3) that necessity is an abstract feature of all
possibility, are helpful for several reasons. In the first
place, the "mysterious character" of possible worlds is dis-
solved: possible worlds are alternative future or once-future
states of *this* world. Indeed, world process is the successive
actualization of possible world after possible world. In the
second place, we now have a metaphysical reason for taking
possibility, rather than necessity, as primitive in modal systems: the necessary is explained in terms of the possible, and

the possible is explained in terms of the future. Finally, the temporal interpretation has a solidly experiential basis: "we experience potentiality as the way in which experience involves the future in the present" (WP, 80-81).

The price to be paid for such an interpretation is that modal logic will have to incorporate the additional (and complicating) factor of time, as in the tense logics of Prior, Hintikka, and Rescher. Possible worlds must be stipulated *relative to* certain times in world process; the metaphysical locus of possibility is, as we have argued, *in actuality* (Chapter II, section 4.2.2). In this sense not everything is possible at a given time, although if something is or once was possible, it will always be true that it was possible.

3.5.2 Individual Identity

In discussing the problem of transworld identity, Alvin Plantinga has suggested an analogy between the transworld and the transtemporal cases: the problem of identifying an individual across possible worlds may be conceived analogously to the problem of identifying the same individual throughout successive temporal phases. What makes the analogy an analogy and not an identity is that "times are linearly ordered," whereas "nothing like this is available in the transworld case."[61]

But obviously if possible worlds *are* temporal states, then we do have an identity and not merely an analogy in the two cases: identity across possible worlds *is* identity through time. So the problem of transworld identity is not one of actually making identifications, for there seems to be little, if any, problem in re-identifying an individual over long periods of time. I may recognize a friend whom I have not seen for many years.

Perhaps the problem is that we cannot intelligibly specify *how* we make the identifications. But we should not let the difficulty of specifying a criterion for identification mask the fact that we do regularly make such identifications. As Linsky points out, "our inability to articulate a clear, explicit, criterion (whatever exactly that is) for the reidentification of individuals through time in the actual world does

not entail our inability to make such reidentifications suc-
cessfully."[62]

Let us examine this question of a criterion more closely.
Specifying a criterion for *identification* depends upon what we
mean by personal or individual *identity*. So our question now
becomes: what is the meaning of individual identity throughout
successive temporal states? For Hartshorne, individual identity is an abstract feature, not a concrete reality (see above,
Chapter II, 2.1). Process philosophy, as we have seen, takes
momentary experiences, actual occasions, as the final metaphysical facts. If concrete experiences are the ultimate actualities, then individual substances are somehow derivative from
them. Indeed, Hartshorne holds (with Whitehead) that substances arise out of experiences in the sense that substances
are abstractions from chains of experiences or event-sequences.
Individual identity, then, is conceived as "genetic identity"
(CS, 185) through successive experiences. There are new selves
in each concrete experience (John-sick, John-well, etc.) so
that "the self as numerically the same is an abstraction, the
latest self as new is the total concrete reality containing the
former" (CS, 184).

A "genetic" theory of identity is to be understood in contrast to a "strict" theory of identity. There are two examples
of strict identity: (1) abstract truths, such as 2 + 2 = 4, and
(2) concrete units of becoming, actual occasions. The criterion of strict identity is that *time does not change the object
referred to*. It will always be true, *simpliciter*, that 2 + 2 =
4, and it will always be true that event x happened at time t;
for example, it will always be true that I just wrote these
words. And note, only (2), that is, only actual occasions, are
both strictly identical and concrete; no *other* form of identity
can be both strict and concrete. My identity, for example, is
not concrete, but is an abstraction from a class or genus of
concrete strict identities. The genetic identity itself is
abstract.

Ordinary language employs this distinction between abstract
identity and concrete states. If I say, for example, "I am
dizzy," I am referring to my present condition, and *only* to that

condition. The statement is obviously nonsensical if it is taken as referring to my identity. On the other hand, if I say, "I am a theologian," I am referring not to a concrete state, but to an abstract identity which is a feature of many concrete states over many years.

We can formalize Hartshorne's genetic theory of identity as follows: let A and B refer to two successive concrete states in a man's life, A being temporally prior to B. B is thus *internally* related to A (i.e., B's occurrence depends upon the occurrence of A), while A is *externally* related to B (A's occurrence is datum for some--though not necessarily *B's*--future occurrence). In much the same way I am internally related to my father, while he is externally related to me, although internally related to *his* father. There will be both an abstract element of identity and concrete elements of diversity in the two states, A and B, the diversity accounting for the different states from which the identity of the man is abstracted. Let I (for "Identity") stand for whatever is the same in the two states and in all others, actual or possible, from which the genetic identity of *this* man is abstracted. Then let us label all the accidental features of each state--i.e., those qualities or relations that are not features of I--by numbers. Thus:

A = (I: 1,2,3,4)
B = (I: 1,2,5,6)

The parentheses symbolize the concrete unity of each state, a unity which includes both a permanent identity and momentary accidents. On the genetic theory of identity, then, the identity of an individual is *in* the concrete states, rather than their being in it. Thus each successive state is the man now, containing in its present concrete fullness all the past states of the man's life *and* the individual abstract identity which runs through all those states. Thus, to complete our formal representation, we should write:

B = [(I: 1,2,5,6) ((I: 1,2,3,4))]

"The double parentheses indicate that the enclosed factors are present only as B's past, as antecedent background; relegated to a subordinate role as merely remembered, rather than now enacted."[63]

The advantage of this analysis is that it explains individual identity as a specific form of causality in general: "genetic identity is a special strand of the causal order of the world, and rests on the same principle of inheritance from the past as causality in general does" (CS, 185). Theories of identity wherein individual substances are regarded as the final metaphysical facts, rather than as abstractions from the final facts, cannot avail themselves of this principle that "the problems of substance and of causality are essentially the same problem" (CS, 185). For where substances are taken as the final concrete facts, individual identity will be misread as a concrete fact, and thus we will be unable to account for identity in terms of something more basic. I will call any explanation which views substances as the final facts, or which holds that accidental changes are "in" substances, rather than vice versa, or which makes individual identity both strict and concrete (rather than genetic and abstract), a *substance* theory of identity. The point of difference between a substance theory and a genetic theory of identity is the answer to the question, what are the final determinate actualities--individual substances or momentary experiences? Hartshorne insists that "the search for the concrete subject must go not only beyond the species to the individual case, in the ordinary meaning of individual thing or person, but a step further, to the temporally as well as the spatially individual case. This is the state or event" (CS, 189). In this way, "we get rid of the suggestion that a single event is adjectival, an abstracted aspect of something more concrete" (CS, 185). Thus Hartshorne can explain individual identity as an abstract feature of the more basic units of becoming which are temporally related. But in substance theories, individuals already *are* the final irreducible units, and so their identity is just given as a brute fact unanalyzable into further components. Whitehead has called this "the fallacy of misplaced concreteness."

This explains why, on substance theories, such questions as whether Nixon could have been a twelfth-century theologian seem so perplexing and so frustrating. We simply have no way of dealing with these puzzles, because when Nixon--and hence his identity--is interpreted as a concrete fact, we have nothing more fundamental to fall back upon in counterfactual situations. Concrete facts *are* the fundamental facts. To generalize: the whole subject of cross-identification suffers at the hands of philosophies of substance as soon as the question of counter-factuals is introduced.

Thus far I have argued that the temporal interpretation of possible worlds means that the problem of transworld identity is not one of actually *making* identifications (for we always re-identify individuals through time), but--at most--a problem of specifying a criterion for identification. I have argued, further, that specifying a criterion for identification depends in large part upon what we mean by individual *identity*. Finally, I have argued that a substance theory of individual identity is *in principle* handicapped in the search for a criterion, whereas an event-theory is able to situate the search in a wider matrix--that of causally efficacious temporal units of becoming.

Not only does the genetic theory allow us to specify the meaning of individual identity in terms of the abstract features that causally connect a series of concrete states, that theory is also required both by the logic of the notion of "identity" and by the temporal interpretation of possible worlds. A comparison of Hartshorne's interpretation of identity with that of Arthur Prior will illustrate the two points. As we have seen, Prior agrees with Hartshorne that possible worlds are to be given a temporal interpretation, so that modal logic is the logic of temporality. But Prior takes issue with Hartshorne's explanation of substantial identity in terms of an abstraction from concrete events. Prior argues, contra Hartshorne, that "chronological language" is to be accommodated to substance language, rather than vice versa:

> To rest content with "chronological" language as it stands would be to abandon the whole enterprise, which is one of the things that makes tensed predicate logic philosophically interesting, of exhibiting events and processes which are ordered and extended in time, and which can be conceived as having "temporal parts," as logical constructions out of persisting and acting things or continuants....it is one

and the same thing (the whole thing, so far as talk of parts and wholes is appropriate here) which at one time does or undergoes this and at another does or undergoes that, and at one time stands here and at another time--by which time it (the same thing) *has stood* here--stands there. It is within this framework that we must try to give the language of "chronology" its meaning; not vice versa.[64]

Thus, as Prior writes elsewhere, this approach requires "falling back on a metaphysic of 'substances' endowed with capacities and dispositions, and our line of escape would hardly be open to someone (let us say Professor Hartshorne) who believes that objects are logical constructions out of events rather than vice versa."[65]

But can Prior's interpretation explain, *logically* explain, individual identity? Hartshorne writes: "'Identity,' in the strictest meaning, connotes entire sameness, total non-difference, in what is said to be identical."[66] Therefore, it is logically incorrect to explain individual identity as that in which changes or accidental qualities inhere, for the changeless cannot include the changing. Clearly the subject of predication is not the individual as identical from moment to moment, but precisely as *not* identical; for only insofar as it is not identical is the contradiction removed in affirming, for example, both red and not-red of it. Therefore, logically (as well as metaphysically) speaking, the subject of predication must be the concrete changing states, and identity must be a function of these states, rather than vice versa.

Furthermore, the substance interpretation of identity is inconsistent with the temporal interpretation of possible worlds. Consider an example: John was well yesterday, but he is sick today. On the substance interpretation of identity, the only way to remove the contradiction between John-well and John-sick is to treat the two predicates, well-then and sick-now, as temporal modifications of the same subject. This does indeed remove the contradiction, but only at the price of regarding the two temporal states as states of the *same* subject. "Yet there is a contradiction in affirming that two moments of process, two events, are but constituents of an identical subject. For while space is the order of co-existence or

co-actuality, time is the order of actualization, of
potentiality-actuality; and this is negated by holding that
there is just one actuality for successive events."[67] In other
words, the only way that two predicates can be in the *same* subject is spatially: John-now is both green (in his eyes) and red
(in his hair). But John-well and John-sick are *temporally* distinct actualities; therefore, sick-now and well-then cannot
both be actual in the same subject. In short, the substance
interpretation of identity entails a spatial understanding of
time (the co-existence of temporal states in the same subject)
which is inconsistent with a temporal understanding (the cumulative actualization, by successive *new* subjects, of possibilities). Therefore, although Prior speaks of possible worlds as
outcomes of actual process, thus adopting a temporal interpretation of time as the actualization of possibility, the theory
he invokes to explain identity across these possible worlds
supposes, quite inconsistently, a *spatial* interpretation of
time. A more consistent view is provided by Hartshorne's genetic theory of identity, according to which John-well and John-
sick are different concrete subjects, and John-as-identical is
an abstract feature of these concrete states.

To summarize: specifying a criterion for identification
across possible worlds depends upon the meaning of individual
identity. Individual identity is best understood according to
Hartshorne's genetic theory: identity is an abstraction from an
event-sequence or chain of concrete experiences. The advan-
tages of this interpretation are three: (1) it explains identity in terms of the more general law of causality; (2) it explains identity in accord with the logical rule that the
changing can include the changeless; (3) it coheres with the
temporal interpretation of possible worlds. The meaning of
individual identity, thus interpreted, is the "essential integrity" or "connectedness of memory and purpose through successive experiences" (CS, 223). The criterion for identification
across possible worlds, then, is not something mysterious and
inexplicable; it is, rather, the specification of those abstract features of a man's identity which have been included in
all his past experiences and must be included in all his future

experiences. In short, it is a man's *essential properties* which serve to identify him from possible world to possible world.

3.5.3 Essential Properties

Quine's attack on quantified modal logic, as we have seen, is that quantification into modal contexts commits one to a doctrine of essential properties. But such a doctrine would seem to be meaningless, and our inability to handle intelligibly such questions as, Could Nixon have been a twelfth-century theologian?, betrays a fundamental confusion in the very notion of essential properties which (supposedly) should serve to identify an individual in counterfactual situations. On the Hartshornean interpretation that I am proposing, however, essential properties can be explained intelligibly, and they can serve to identify an individual across possible worlds. The interpretive key for understanding essential properties is the same key used to understand possible worlds and individual identity, *viz.*, the notion of causally efficacious temporal units of becoming.

Consider the following diagram:

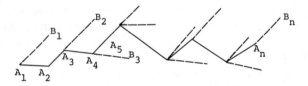

The points, $A_1 \ldots A_n$, represent the momentary experiences that make up an individual's history or career. The solid line *is* the individual, and as such is a shorthand or simplification for the abstract identity connecting the concrete experiences as experiences of this man. The dotted lines represent alternative future or once-future possibilities for actualization. They are paths to the various possible worlds, $B_1 \ldots B_n$.

The principle of the whole diagram is *creative freedom within the context of temporal inheritance*. For example, the possibilities at A_2 lie within the confines of what is inherited from A_1, A_3 depends on A_2 in the same way, and so forth.

Possibilities are rooted in the actualities which precede them.
At any point several future possibilities are open, and freedom
consists in actualizing just this possibility rather than that.
But at no point is something really possible unless it is in
conformation to the causally inherited past.

Possible worlds, individual identity, and essential properties are all to be understood in this context of causality--
this is, I am suggesting, precisely the superiority of Hartshorne's analysis. Essential properties are those abstract features which constitute individual identity and which must be
included by every future possibility which could be actualized
as a state in which *this* individual exists. What must be inherited by every alternative future in which an individual
might exist is an essential property of the individual. *Essential properties are causally efficacious boundaries for individual development.*

Obvious candidates for such properties include being human
or being born at such-and-such a time. Thus, Nixon could *not*
have been a twelfth-century theologian, because his birth in
this century means that all subsequent experiences which constitute "Nixon" must conform to his being born at such-and-such
a time. Not that Nixon's birth was necessary, but *his* birth
supposes that we have a chain of experiences sufficiently developed to abstract an individual identity--"him"--from them.
It is nonsense to ask if this entire sequence could have taken
place at another time, for it would no longer be *this* temporal
sequence. Identity, once again, is chiefly a retrospective
abstraction from a route of temporal occasions. To relocate
the temporality is to change the individual.

We must also allow for the *emergence* of essential properties in an individual's career. Say, for example, that A_3 entails the origin of a novel property which *then* must be incor-
porated by every subsequent entity. Thus, after a certain
point, it may be an essential property of Nixon that he is a
politician and not a theologian. So when we are stipulating
counterfactuals, we must specify what point in an individual's
life we are talking about. This specification of essential
properties may be complicated, but it is not unintelligible or
nonsensical.

114

4. Summary

Hartshorne has argued that in the ontological proof modality *de dicto* and modality *de re* are coextensive, which is to say that the existence of God, in addition to being a logically necessary truth, is also an ontologically necessary feature of reality. In this chapter I have outlined what I consider to be the three chief objections to this theory of modality, and I have suggested that Quine's attack on the intelligibility of *de re* modality constitutes the most serious threat to the modal aspect of Hartshorne's ontological proof. I have therefore taken a rather long detour to discuss the logical, semantical, and metaphysical aspects of Quine's challenge. Quine's contention is, finally, that the semantics required by *de re* modality (a possible world semantics, such as Kripke's) involves the proponent of *de re* modality in a nonsensical metaphysical position, "Aristotelian essentialism," to use Quine's phrase. The problem of transworld identity is used to illustrate the point.

I have argued that Hartshorne's metaphysics provides the principles for an alternative interpretation of Kripke's possible world semantics, an interpretation that does not run into the problems of "Aristotelian essentialism." According to this Hartshornean interpretation, possible worlds, individual identity and essential properties (collectively, the problem of transworld identity) can be examined and understood under the one principle of temporal inheritance or causality. Or, in short, *temporal process* is the interpretive key to *de re* modality. What is unintelligible or nonsensical is not *de re* necessity, but a substance interpretation of *de re* necessity. I conclude that Hartshorne's use of modality *de re* is not only required by the ontological proof, but is justified as well by the process metaphysics which supports that proof.

CHAPTER IV

[1]Charles Hartshorne, "Rationale of the Ontological Proof,"
Theology Today 20/2 (July 1963), p. 279.

[2]Ibid.

[3]John Hick, "A Critique of the 'Second Argument,'" *The
Many-Faced Argument*, ed. John H. Hick and Arthur C. McGill (New
York: Macmillan, 1967), p. 350.

[4]Ibid., p. 349.

[5]Ibid., p. 351; italics added.

[6]Ibid.

[7]Ibid., p. 349.

[8]Ibid., p. 348.

[9]W. Donald Hudson, *A Philosophical Approach to Religion*
(London: Barnes & Noble, 1974), p. 36.

[10]Ibid., p. 37.

[11]John Hick, "A Critique of the 'Second Argument,'" p. 349.

[12]Hartshorne, "Rationale of the Ontological Proof," p. 281.

[13]Ibid., p. 279.

[14]Ibid., p. 282.

[15]Hartshorne, "Necessity," p. 291.

[16]Hartshorne, "Real Possibility," pp. 596-97.

[17]Hartshorne, "Rationale of the Ontological Proof," p. 279.

[18]Hartshorne, "Real Possibility," p. 598.

[19]Hartshorne, "Rationale of the Ontological Proof," p. 282.

[20]Leonard Linsky, "Reference, Essentialism, and Modality,"
in *Reference and Modality*, ed. Leonard Linsky (London: Oxford
University, 1971), pp. 89-90.

[21]W. V. O. Quine, "Reference and Modality," in *From a
Logical Point of View*, 2nd ed. (New York: Harper and Row, 1963),
p. 145.

116

[22]Alvin Plantinga, *The Nature of Necessity* (Oxford: Clarendon, 1974), p. 227.

[23]Quine, "Reference and Modality," p. 139.

[24]Linsky, "Reference, Essentialism, and Modality," p. 89.

[25]Ibid., p. 90.

[26]Quine, "Reference and Modality," p. 148.

[27]Ibid.

[28]Ibid.

[29]Plantinga, *The Nature of Necessity*, pp. 224-27.

[30]Ibid., p. 229.

[31]Arthur F. Smullyan, "Modality and Description," in Linsky, *Reference and Modality*, pp. 35-43.

[32]Ibid., p. 39.

[33]Quine, "Reference and Modality," p. 155.

[34]Ibid.

[35]Ibid.

[36]Ibid., p. 143

[37]Ibid., p. 149.

[38]G. E. Hughes and M. J. Cresswell, *An Introduction to Modal Logic* (London: Methuen & Co., 1968), p. 23.

[39]Plantinga, *The Nature of Necessity*, p. 223.

[40]Linsky, "Reference, Essentialism, and Modality," p. 95.

[41]David Braine, *Mind* 77/307 (July 1968), p. 448.

[42]Hartshorne, "Rationale of the Ontological Proof," p. 279.

[43]Hartshorne, "Necessity," p. 291.

[44]Hartshorne, "Rationale of the Ontological Proof," p. 279.

[45]Hughes and Cresswell, *An Introduction to Modal Logic*, pp. 184-85.

[46]Saul A. Kripke, "Semantical Considerations on Modal Logic," in Linsky, *Reference and Modality*, pp. 63-72.

[47]Ibid., p. 64.

[48] Ibid.

[49] Ibid., p. 65.

[50] Ibid., pp. 66-67.

[51] Ibid., p. 67.

[52] Plantinga, *The Nature of Necessity*, p. 92.

[53] Ibid., p. 93.

[54] *Words and Objections: Essays on the Work of W. V. Quine*, ed. D. Davidson and Jaakko Hintikka (Dordrecht: D. Reidel, 1969), p. 338.

[55] Jaakko Hintikka, "The Semantics of Modal Notions and the Indeterminacy of Ontology," in *Semantics of Natural Language*, ed. Donald Davidson and Gilbert Harman (Dordrecht: D. Reidel, 1972), p. 411.

[56] Quine, "Reference and Modality," p. 156.

[57] Linsky, "Reference, Essentialism, and Modality," p. 99. By a "metaphysical" problem, Linsky means the problem of not having "a clear, explicit, intuitive, understanding of a semantics such as Kripke's" (ibid.).

[58] Saul Kripke, "Naming and Necessity," in *Semantics of Natural Language*, ed. Donald Davidson and Gilbert Harman (Dordrecht: D. Reidel, 1972), p. 267.

[59] Ibid., p. 345, n. 15.

[60] Arthur N. Prior, *Papers on Time and Tense* (Oxford: Clarendon, 1968), p. 69.

[61] Plantinga, *The Nature of Necessity*, p. 95.

[62] Linsky, "Reference, Essentialism, and Modality," p. 99.

[63] Charles Hartshorne, "Strict and Genetic Identity: An Illustration of the Relations of Logic to Metaphysics," in *Structure, Method, and Meaning: Essays in Honor of Henry M. Sheffer*, ed. Paul Henle, Horace M. Kallen, Susanne K. Langer (New York: Liberal Arts Press, 1951), p. 248.

[64] Prior, *Papers on Time and Tense*, p. 86.

[65] Ibid., p. 64.

[66] Hartshorne, "Strict and Genetic Identity," p. 242.

[67] Ibid., p. 251.

A SUMMARY OF THE ARGUMENT

The interior logic of Hartshorne's ontological proof, as I argued in Chapter I, is an exploitation of the insight that with necessary things, to be possible and to be are the same. Symbolically, $(q \rightarrow \Box q) \supset (\Diamond q \rightarrow q)$. A possibly necessary truth *is* a necessary truth. One of the purposes of this study has been to focus discussion of the proof where it ought to be focused: on the central assumption that the existence of God is possible. The *possibility* of the divine existence is the issue at issue in the proof. What we mean by "possible" is thus the crux of the ontological question.

In this regard, Hartshorne has made two important claims: (1) that the ontological proof may legitimately or plausibly assume[1] the *logical* possibility of the divine existency by appealing to a genuinely conceivable neoclassical interpretation of God (in this way it demonstrates the logical *necessity* of the divine existence); (2) that the proof may legitimately assume the *real* possibility of the divine existence by appealing to the theory of modal correspondence outlined in Chapter IV (in this way it demonstrates the real *necessity* of the divine existence). According to Hartshorne, the proof permits --indeed demands--a *de re* as well as a *de dicto* interpretation. Not only is the existence of God a logically necessary truth, God also has the essential property of necessary existence. Or, symbolically, $\Box (\exists x) Px . \supset . (\exists x) \Box Px$.

Opponents of the proof have made parallel counterclaims: (1) The proof may not legitimately assume the logical possibility (and hence does not prove the logical necessity) of the divine existence, *either* (a) because the idea of God is nonsensical *or* (b) because the incomprehensible mystery of God transcends rational analysis. (2) The proof may not legitimately assume the real possibility (and hence does not establish the real necessity) of the divine existence, *either* (a) because the idea of *de re* modality is nonsensical *or* (b) because logical or linguistic modalities do not correspond to real or ontological modalities.

The twofold thesis of this study has been: (1) that the success of Hartshorne's ontological proof does indeed depend upon the conceivability of divinity and upon a theory of modal correspondence between logical possibility and necessity and ontological possibility and necessity; and (2) that both the theory of divinity and the theory of modality are specifications of Hartshorne's metaphysics of temporal possibility. I support the proof because I support the metaphysical interpretation of possibility upon which it depends. Let me review the evidence, using as a convenient organizational scheme the objections to the proof.

Objection 1a: The notion of a divine being is nonsensical, and hence is not a logically possible idea. *Reply*: The question of the conceivability of God is the question of the conceivability of a necessary existent. That such a being must be conceivable may be argued as follows: (1) Creative synthesis, or process, is the ultimate principle of all reality. There is no conceivable alternative to process (Chapter II, 2.2). (2) Process demands potentiality: "the reality of creativity is the very basis of possibility or potentiality itself" (CS, 264). Possibility is process in its forward or creative aspect (Chapter II, 4.2.1). That there should be possibility is thus not itself a possibility, but is an unconditionally necessary existential truth. (3) Possibilities must have actual antecedents; the metaphysical locus of possibility is in actuality (Chapter II, 4.2.2). "What is possible next is simply what is compatible with what has happened up to now" (CS, 68). (4) Every actuality is a concrete instance of abstract individual existence (the existence of socially ordered sequences of actualities). Possibility, therefore, is a feature of existing individuals. (5) If the ground of possibility itself is unconditionally necessary, then not everything that exists can be contingent, else the being of possibility would also be contingent, and it might have been that nothing was possible.[2] Therefore, there must be one necessarily-existing individual whose being is co-extensive with potentiality itself. The idea of a necessary existent is required by process itself.

Objection 1b: The essence of God is ultimately mysterious and unknowable by finite minds. In this sense, God cannot be conceived, and so is not a logical possibility. *Reply*: The essence of God is unknowable only on the assumption that the mystery of God refers to the whole reality of God, a reality where essence equals existence--period. On the contrary, the abstract essence-existence of God must be abstracted *from* something, namely, concrete divine states (Chapter III, 4.1). Necessary existence means the necessary non-emptiness of the class of contingent concrete states. This existence-actuality distinction allows us to specify coherently where the divine mystery lies: not in the abstract existence which may be conceived as modally coextensive with all that is actual as actual and with all that is possible as possible, but in the concrete fullness, which, like all concrete actualities, resists rational analysis. The ontological argument does not encroach upon the mystery of God; it shows, rather, that the mystery necessarily exists.

Objection 2a: The notion of *de re* modality is philosophical nonsense, for the possible world semantics required by quantified modal logic commits us to an unintelligible metaphysics, "Aristotelian essentialism." Our inability to solve the transworld identity problem is evidence that all talk of necessary or essential properties (including, therefore, the essential property of necessary existence) is meaningless. *Reply*: Hartshorne's metaphysics of temporal possibility provides the principles for an intelligible philosophical interpretation of possible world semantics and therefore of quantified modal logic. The problem of transworld identity is not one of *making* identifications (for we always reidentify individuals throughout time), but of *specifying a criterion* for making the identifications. Using the resources of Hartshorne's metaphysics (resources significantly different from those available in a metaphysics of being), I have argued that we specify this criterion in exactly the same way that we specify possible worlds: according to the laws of internal and external relations (causal efficacy and objective immortality) which characterize all temporal process. Possible worlds are alternative *future* outcomes of the actual world (actuality is thus

externally related to possibility, while possibility is internally related to actuality); individual identity is *genetic*
identity throughout successive temporal states, i.e., it is
that abstract thread of internal relations causally connecting
a whole series of temporal states; essential properties are
those abstract features which collectively constitute individual identity and which must be included in every possible world
whose actualization could serve as a concrete state in which a
particular individual exists. The question of possible worlds
is the question of what could be an *effect* of the actual world;
the question of individual identity is the question of the
causal link connecting a history of actualities; the question
of essential properties is the question of those abstract features which constitute the causal link. *The criterion for
transworld identity is the determination of which possible effects could be instances of this particular causal sequence.*
In principle, then, possible worlds, individual identity and
essential properties are no more mysterious or unintelligible
than the general law of causality.

When Hartshorne says that God has the essential property
of necessary existence, he is saying that the divine existence
is that abstract feature which must be included by any world
that is so much as even possible, that is, by all future or
once-future states of this world; or, alternatively, that there
is no possible future world state which excludes the reality of
God. Or again, there is no possible world state which could
not serve as a concrete instance from which the identity of God
may be abstracted. Being the very ground of alternatives, his
non-existence is not one of the alternatives. We thus return
once again to Hartshorne's thesis that possibility is expressive of the divine, and that the divine existence constitutes
possibility as such.

In sum, what constitutes ontological possibility as such
is ontological necessity, i.e., the necessary existence of God.
If ontological necessity is unintelligible, then futurity (ontological possibility) is also unintelligible.

Objection 2b: Even if *de re* modality makes sense, we cannot assume that a demonstration of the logical possibility

(and--by the ontological proof--of the logical necessity) of the divine existence is *ipso facto* a demonstration of the real possibility (and thus the real necessity) of the divine existence. There is no necessary correlation between modality *de dicto* and modality *de re*. *Reply*: There cannot *fail* to be a correlation between modality *de dicto* and modality *de re*, and, in the case of absolute necessities, the two modalities must be completely coextensive. Again, it is the metaphysics of temporal possibility which provides the supporting evidence for the contention.

Something is possible--really or logically--according to one standard only: compatibility with actuality (Chapter II, 4.2.2). Hartshorne does not equivocate in his use of this term, and indeed we may ask what *else* possibility could mean? To say that a state of affairs is *really* possible is to say that it could be an outcome of the present actual state of the world. To say that an idea is *logically* possible is to say that the meanings involved in the idea do not contradict one another. But meanings must mean something, they must have referents. The minimal requirement for qualification as a "meaning," therefore, is reference to something. But reference to what? Can a meaning refer only to itself? By that standard, *any* thought would be logically possible: the meaning of round square refers to the meaning of round square. Such circularity is nonsense. The meanings of a consistent thought must refer to something other than themselves, namely, to things which *are* actual or to things which *could* be actual. If a meaning refers to "something" that is not even possible, then it refers to literally nothing. The minimal reference of a logical possibility is to a *real* capacity of world process. On the temporal understanding of possible worlds, then, the criterion of logical possibility and the criterion of real possibility are the same. "Meanings are logically possible only because referents are ontologically possible or actual."[3]

We may go further: if an idea is not merely logically *possible*, but logically *necessary* (in the absolute or unconditional sense), its reference is not to a capacity of world process, but to the ultimate *identity* in world process. An absolutely necessary truth, being the abstract feature of *all* alternative future states of the world, must be both *de dicto* and *de re*. If the necessary existence of deity is a coherent idea, to what could it refer except to the identity in ontological process?

In sum, the temporal interpretation of possibility is an argument for the connectedness of modality *de dicto* and modality *de re*: "Not that all thought represents actualities, that is, fully actualized possibilities; rather all thought, not absurd or inconsistent, represents *either* something necessary, which never was merely future, *or* something contingent that once was future."[4]

The replies to the preceding objections are intended to summarize the argument of this study. That argument is both *interpretive*, in that it shows the centrality of the issue of metaphysical possibility to Hartshorne's proof, and *constructive*, in that it employs the principles of Hartshorne's metaphysics to provide an intelligible interpretation of *de re* modality.

It is reasonable to ask, by way of conclusion, if Hartshorne's argument proves the logical and ontological necessity of the divine existence. My answer is yes, in the sense that the proof shows clearly the price involved in rejecting the theistic conclusion, and I have argued that the price is too high to pay. One who would reject the proof must reject one or more of the following five theses, all of which are implicit in, and implied by, the assumption that the existence of God is possible:

    I. "CREATIVE SYNTHESIS OCCURS" IS AN UNCONDITIONALLY NECESSARY EXISTENTIAL TRUTH.

    II. PROCESS DEMANDS POTENTIALITY; THAT THERE BE POSSIBILITIES IS AN UNCONDITIONALLY NECESSARY TRUTH.

    III. POSSIBILITY IS FUTURITY; *ALL* POSSIBILITIES MUST HAVE ACTUAL ANTECEDENTS.

    IV. THE DIVINE EXISTENCE IS CONCEIVABLE *A PRIORI* AS MODAL COEXTENSIVENESS.

    V. INDIVIDUAL IDENTITY IS AN ABSTRACTION FROM CONCRETE STATES.

All of the arguments in this study have been derived from these propositions, propositions, I have argued, whose rejection is counter-intuitive. Taken together, the propositions imply the theistic conclusion.

CHAPTER V

[1]I say plausibly *assume* because, strictly speaking, the ontological proof of itself does not *prove* the possibility of God; this is the task of the other arguments, such as the cosmological. "In this form, in which both the non-impossibility and thence the actuality of God are proved, the argument is no longer merely the ontological, but includes a form of the cosmological as the first step" (MVG, 333). In this way, Hartshorne argues, the theistic proofs strengthen one another at their weakest points: for example, the cosmological argument supports what for the ontological argument is merely an assumption, that deity can be given consistent meaning; conversely, the ontological supports the cosmological at *its* weakest point by showing that if the theistic explanation is genuinely conceivable it must be *uniquely* true. See Hartshorne's article, "Six Theistic Proofs," in *Creative Synthesis and Philosophic Method* for further discussion.

[2]Steps (4) and (5) need clarification and support from some of the other theistic arguments, especially the cosmological and the design arguments, both in somewhat untraditional forms.

[3]Hartshorne, "The Formal Validity and Real Significance of the Ontological Argument," p. 226.

[4]Hartshorne, "Real Possibility," p. 598.

BIBLIOGRAPHY

Works by Charles Hartshorne

Books

Anselm's Discovery: A Re-Examination of the Ontological Argument for the Existence of God. LaSalle, IL: Open Court, 1965.

Beyond Humanism: Essays in the Philosophy of Nature. Chicago: Willett, Clark & Co., 1937; reprint ed., Lincoln: University of Nebraska, 1968.

Creative Synthesis and Philosophic Method. LaSalle, IL: Open Court, 1970.

The Divine Relativity: A Social Conception of God. New Haven and London: Yale University, 1948.

The Logic of Perfection and Other Essays in Neoclassical Metaphysics. LaSalle, IL: Open Court, 1962.

Man's Vision of God and the Logic of Theism. Chicago: Willett, Clark & Co., 1941; reprint ed., Hamden, CT: Archon Books, 1964.

A Natural Theology for Our Time. LaSalle, IL: Open Court, 1967.

Philosophers Speak of God (with William Reese). Chicago: University of Chicago, 1953.

Reality as Social Process: Studies in Metaphysics and Religion. Glencoe, IL: Free Press, 1953; reprint ed., New York: Hafner Publishing Co., 1971.

Whitehead's Philosophy: Selected Essays, 1935-1970. Lincoln: University of Nebraska, 1972.

Articles

"Can There Be Proofs for the Existence of God?" Pp. 62-75 in *Religious Language and Knowledge*. Edited by Robert H. Ayers and William T. Blackstone. Athens: University of Georgia, 1972.

"The Formal Validity and Real Significance of the Ontological Argument." *The Philosophical Review* 3 (May 1944): 225-45.

"Further Fascination of the Ontological Argument: Replies to Richardson." *Union Seminary Quarterly Review* 18 (March 1963): 244-45.

130

"Is the Denial of Existence Ever Contradictory?" *The Journal of Philosophy* 63 (February 1966): 85-93.

"The Logic of the Ontological Argument." *The Journal of Philosophy* 58 (August 1961): 471-73.

"The Logical Structure of Givenness." *The Philosophical Quarterly* 8 (October 1958): 307-16.

"The Meaning of 'Is Going to Be.'" *Mind* 74 (January 1965): 46-58.

"Necessity." *The Review of Metaphysics* 21 (December 1967): 290-96.

"On Hartshorne's Formulation of the Ontological Argument: A Rejoinder." *The Philosophical Review* 54 (January 1945): 63-65.

"Rationale of the Ontological Proof." *Theology Today* 20 (July 1963): 278-83.

"Real Possibility." *The Journal of Philosophy* 60 (October 1963): 593-605.

"Rejoinder to Purtill." *The Review of Metaphysics* 21 (December 1967): 308-9.

"Santayana's Doctrine of Essence." Pp. 137-82 in *The Philosophy of George Santayana*. Edited by Paul A. Schilpp. New York: Tudor Publishing Co., 1940.

"Strict and Genetic Identity: An Illustration of the Relations of Logic to Metaphysics." Pp. 242-54 in *Structure, Method, and Meaning: Essays in Honor of Henry M. Sheffer*. Edited by Paul Henle, Horace M. Kallen, and Suzanne K. Langer. New York: Liberal Arts Press, 1951.

"The Theistic Proofs." *Union Seminary Quarterly Review* 20 (January 1965): 115-29.

"What Did Anselm Discover?" *Union Seminary Quarterly Review* 17 (March 1962): 213-22.

Other Sources

Anselm. *St. Anselm: Basic Writings*. Translated by S. N. Deane. Introduction by Charles Hartshorne. 2d ed. LaSalle, IL: Open Court, 1968.

Aquinas, Thomas. *Summa Theologica*. Vol. I, First Part. Translated by Fathers of the English Dominican Province. New York: Benziger Brothers, 1947.

Audet, T. A. "Une Source Augustinienne de l'Argument de Saint
    Anselme." Pp. 105-42 in *Etienne Gilson, Philosophe de la
    Chrétienté*. Edited by J. Maritain. Paris: Editions du
    Cerf, 1949.

Barnes, Jonathan. *The Ontological Argument*. New York: Mac-
    millan, 1972.

Braine, David. "Review of *Anselm's Discovery*, by Charles
    Hartshorne." *Mind* 77 (July 1968): 447-50.

Carnap, Rudolf. *Meaning and Necessity*. Chicago: University of
    Chicago, 1947.

Cohen, Morris R., and Nagel, Ernest. *An Introduction to Logic*.
    New York: Harcourt, Brace & World, 1934; Harbinger Books,
    1962.

Cohen, Morris R. *A Preface to Logic*. New York: Meridian Books,
    1956.

Davidson, D., and Hintikka, Jaakko, eds. *Words and Objections:
    Essays on the Work of W. V. Quine*. Dordrecht: D. Reidel,
    1969.

Findlay, J. N. "Can God's Existence Be Disproved?" *Mind* 57
    (1948): 176-83.

_____. "Reflections on Necessary Existence." Pp. 515-27 in
    Process and Divinity: The Hartshorne Festschrift. Edited
    by William L. Reese and Eugene Freeman. LaSalle, IL: Open
    Court, 1964.

Flew, Antony. *God and Philosophy*. New York: Dell, 1966.

_____, and MacIntyre, Alasdair, eds. *New Essays in Philo-
    sophical Theology*. New York: Macmillan, 1955; Macmillan
    Paperbacks, 1964.

Ford, Lewis S., ed. *Two Process Philosophers: Hartshorne's
    Encounter with Whitehead*. AAR Studies in Religion 5.
    Missoula: University of Montana, 1973.

Hick, John H., and McGill, Arthur C., eds. *The Many-Faced
    Argument*. New York: Macmillan, 1967.

Hintikka, Jaakko. "The Semantics of Modal Notions and the
    Indeterminacy of Ontology." Pp. 398-414 in *Semantics of
    Natural Language*. Edited by Donald Davidson and Gilbert
    Harman. 2d ed. Dordrecht: D. Reidel, 1972.

Hudson, W. Donald. *A Philosophical Approach to Religion*.
    London: Barnes & Noble, 1974.

Hughes, G. E., and Cresswell, M. J. *An Introduction to Modal
    Logic*. London: Methuen, 1968; University Paperbacks, 1972.

Kant, Immanuel. *Critique of Pure Reason*. Translated by Norman Kemp Smith. London: Macmillan, 1970.

Kneale, W. "Modality De Dicto and De Re." Pp. 622-33 in *Logic, Methodology and Philosophy of Science*. Edited by Ernest Nagel, Patrick Suppes, and Alfred Tarsk. Stanford, CA: Stanford University, 1962.

Koyré, Alexandre. *L'Idée de Dieu dans la Philosophie de St. Anselme*. Paris: Editions Ernest Leroux, 1923.

Kripke, Saul A. "Naming and Necessity." Pp. 253-355 in *Semantics of Natural Language*. Edited by Donald Davidson and Gilbert Harman. 2d ed. Dordrecht: D. Reidel, 1972.

_____. "Semantical Considerations on Modal Logic." Pp. 63-72 in *Reference and Modality*. Edited by Leonard Linsky. London: Oxford University, 1971.

Leclerc, Ivor. *Whitehead's Metaphysics: An Introductory Exposition*. London: George Allen & Unwin, 1958.

Linsky, Leonard, ed. *Reference and Modality*. London: Oxford University, 1971.

_____. *Referring*. London: Routledge & Kegan Paul, 1967.

Malcolm, Norman. "Anselm's Ontological Arguments." *Philosophical Review* 69 (1960): 41-62.

Martin, R. M. *The Notion of Analytic Truth*. Philadelphia: University of Pennsylvania, 1959.

_____. *Whitehead's Categoreal Scheme and Other Papers*. The Hague: Martinus Nijhoff, 1974.

Nelson, J. O. "Modal Logic and the Ontological Proof for God's Existence." *The Review of Metaphysics* 17 (1963): 235-42.

Ogden, Schubert M. *The Reality of God and Other Essays*. New York: Harper & Row, 1963.

Plantinga, Alvin. *God, Freedom, and Evil*. New York: Harper & Row, 1974.

_____. *The Nature of Necessity*. Oxford: Clarendon, 1974.

_____, ed. *The Ontological Argument*. New York: Doubleday, 1965.

Prior, Arthur N. *Papers on Time and Tense*. Oxford: Clarendon, 1968.

_____. *Time and Modality*. Oxford: Clarendon, 1957.

Purtill, Richard L. "Hartshorne's Modal Proof." *The Journal of Philosophy* 63 (July 1966): 397-409.

_____. *Logic for Philosophers*. New York: Harper & Row, 1971.

_____. "Ontological Modalities." *The Review of Metaphysics* 21 (December 1967): 297-307.

Quine, W. V. O. *From a Logical Point of View*. 2d ed. New York: Harper & Row, 1963.

_____. *The Ways of Paradox*. New York: Random House, 1966.

Rescher, Nicholas, and Urquhart, Alasdair. *Temporal Logic*. New York: Springer Verlag, 1971.

Rescher, Nicholas. *Topics in Philosophical Logic*. Dordrecht: D. Reidel, 1968.

Ross, James F. *Introduction to the Philosophy of Religion*. London: Macmillan, 1969.

_____. "On Proofs for the Existence of God." Pp. 1-19 in *Logical Analysis and Contemporary Theism*. Edited by John Donnelly. New York: Fordham University, 1972.

Russell, Bertrand. "On Denoting." *Mind* 14 (1905).

Sleigh, R. C. *Necessary Truth*. Englewood Cliffs, NJ: Prentice Hall, 1972.

Smith, John E. *Experience and God*. New York: Oxford University, 1968.

Smullyan, Arthur F. "Modality and Description." Pp. 35-43 in *Reference and Modality*. Edited by Leonard Linsky. London: Oxford University, 1971.

Tillich, Paul. *Systematic Theology*. Vol. I. Chicago: University of Chicago, 1951.

_____. "The Two Types of Philosophy of Religion." Pp. 10-29 in *Theology of Culture*. Edited by Robert C. Kimball. New York: Oxford University, 1964.

Whitehead, Alfred North. *Adventures of Ideas*. New York: Macmillan, 1933; Free Press Paperback, 1967.

_____. *Modes of Thought*. New York: Macmillan, 1938; Free Press Paperback, 1968.

_____. *Process and Reality*. New York: Macmillan, 1929; Free Press Paperback, 1969.